Brainstorms and Blueprints

Brainstorms and Blueprints
Teaching Library Research as a Thinking Process

Barbara K. Stripling and
Judy M. Pitts

1988

Libraries Unlimited, Inc.   Englewood, Colorado

LIBRARIES UNLIMITED, INC.
P.O. Box 6633
Englewood, CO 80155-6633

Library of Congress Cataloging-in-Publication Data

Stripling, Barbara K.
 Brainstorms and blueprints : teaching library research as a
thinking process / Barbara K. Stripling and Judy M. Pitts.
  xv, 181 p. 22x28 cm.
  Bibliography: p. 171
  Includes index.
  ISBN 0-87287-638-1
  1. High school students--Library orientation. 2. Research-
-Methodology--Study and teaching (Secondary) 3. Report writing-
-Study and teaching (Secondary) I. Pitts, Judy M. II. Title.
Z711.2.S75 1988
025.5'678'223--dc19   88-12821
                                                            CIP

TABLE OF CONTENTS

LIST OF HANDOUTS

PREFACE

Exciting. Interesting. Mind-involving. Stimulating. Thought-provoking. Library research projects in secondary schools should be *all* of the above; too often they are *none* of the above.

Dull research assignments exist because students often do not *think* about their research. Instead they use simple library skills to find a few sources, scribble some haphazard notes, and piece together a paper as if it were a jigsaw puzzle. Their own thoughts and conclusions are missing from the whole process.

This book provides creative strategies (brainstorms) and logical processes (blueprints) for secondary teachers and library media specialists who want to break the mindless research cycle by teaching library research as a thinking process.

Research can be performed at different levels of thought, from simply finding facts to generating new concepts about complex issues. A *research taxonomy* delineates six levels of thought for research assignments.

Students also must think about the products that they develop based on their research. Their reactions may vary from simply recalling the information to creating a project that communicates original ideas. A *REACTS taxonomy* depicts the different levels of reactions, and creative assignments are offered for each level of the taxonomy.

Once the thought levels of the research and reactions are established, a ten-step *research process* provides the structure for conducting research as a thinking process. Skills, strategies, and activities for teaching the process are included with each step.

Students who learn the brainstorms and blueprints of research gain powerful, lifelong, information skills.

The authors would like to express appreciation to the teachers at Fayetteville High School, Fayetteville, Arkansas, many of whom endlessly inspire us, and to the district's administration, which encourages us to excel. We would especially like to thank Don B. Deweese, our "boss" and friend who is always ready to help, and Dr. David Loertscher, who made us believe this book was possible. We dedicate this book to our families who have deferred their own priorities to our dream.

Chapter 1

RESEARCH AS A THINKING PROCESS

One spring afternoon Mr. Peterson, the high school library media specialist, noticed Julie slouched against the bookcase, thumbing through several volumes of the *World Book* encyclopedia. Detecting frustration behind Julie's bored demeanor, Mr. Peterson offered assistance.

"Can I help you find anything?"

"I have to find something I can copy for my biology report on an animal."

"What animal are you interested in?"

"Oh, I don't care. I just have to get this done. I guess I'll do bears," sighed the reluctant student.

"How about picking an unusual animal that you don't know much about, like the aardvark or whooping crane? You never know, you might learn something."

"I don't want to learn anything, I just want to get this done for biology credit."

"O.K., I'll help you find something on bears. Let's start with the index." Mr. Peterson had learned to be gallant in defeat.

LIBRARY RESEARCH

The Brown-Bear-Is-Brown Disease

Many students, like Julie, are afflicted with the "Brown-Bear-Is-Brown" disease. The first symptoms are that students pick a research subject about which there can be little difference of opinion and about which they care nothing ("the brown bear"). Second they go to one source (preferably a general encyclopedia) to find information; when they arrive at the shelf they pull only one book from it (not the index, just the "B" volume). Finally, they refuse to delve deeper than the surface information; whatever they find, they copy without thinking ("the brown bear is brown").

The treatment for the "Brown-Bear-Is-Brown" disease is teaching students to think while they are researching. A Japanese proverb says that if you give a man a fish, he will be fed for a day, but if you teach a man to fish, he will be fed for a lifetime. Today's corollary is that if you teach a man to *think* about his fishing, he might invent a technique that would feed a whole town beyond his lifetime. At the very least, he won't hook any brown bears while he's fishing.

Students have varying degrees of thinking skills. The mistake has been in assuming that they can improve those skills by observing and imitating others' thinking. Instead, students must be taught, in every area of the curriculum, how to think more effectively.

Teachers and library media specialists have many tools for teaching students to think—special teaching strategies, learning strategies, and subject matter. One effective strategy for encouraging thinking in any subject area is teaching students to perform thoughtful library research.

Why Is Library Research Important?

In the library media center, students can learn to use both creative and critical thinking, the brainstorms and blueprints of library research. Students who learn to handle information both creatively and critically in the library will be able to use the same skills in classroom activities.

Library research offers rewards for everyone involved—teachers, library media specialists, and students—if the research connects with the classroom learning or answers a student's personal needs.

Teachers who integrate library research into classroom activities recognize that research expands the boundaries of learning which may be limited by textbooks. The information in textbooks is often several years old and watered down to make it acceptable throughout the country. Library research allows teachers to concentrate on current, controversial, or local issues not included in the textbook or to devise in-depth units on topics covered only briefly.

Library media specialists recognize that research units offer an opportunity to expose students to library materials and to teach library skills in a context in which they will be used and remembered. When students *need* research skills, they are receptive to them.

Students also profit from library research units. Research helps students learn the lifelong "blueprint skills" of information use—how to seek, find, and use ideas independently. Research also helps students acquire the "brainstorm skills"—how to develop new, research-based concepts and how to present their findings in creative, effective formats.

Considerations in Planning a Research Unit

An important predictor of success in student library research is the thoroughness of the planning by library media specialists and classroom teachers. Although no "Rules to Plan Research Units By" will guarantee thoughtful student research, library media specialists and teachers should consider two aspects when planning a library unit: (1) the thought level of the research, and (2) the type and level of product the student must create as a reaction to research. If both of these features are built into the research assignment, the library media specialist and teacher can predetermine the thought level and quality of the entire research project.

Thoughtful *research* involves critical, and sometimes creative, thinking skills; the research may be performed at a variety of levels from simple fact-finding to complex conceptualizing. Thoughtful *reactions* also involve both critical and creative thinking skills and may vary from simple recalling to complex synthesizing.

The levels of thoughtful research and thoughtful reactions to research can be visualized on taxonomies. Students should begin at the lowest level of the taxonomies (the simplest research and reactions). As the students practice and build their skills, they may be led to higher levels of each taxonomy.

TAXONOMY OF THOUGHTFUL RESEARCH

Fact-finding

Asking / Searching

Examining / Organizing

Evaluating / Deliberating

Integrating / Concluding

Conceptualizing

The levels of the taxonomy represent a progression in depth of thinking about the research. Students start at the fact-finding level in the elementary grades. Their progress through the taxonomy depends on individual abilities and on the amount of practice they are given. Students who are given several research experiences at each grade level will advance more rapidly than those who are only occasionally assigned research projects.

A districtwide plan of library research will help students move through the taxonomy. Although the plan will differ in each school district, a possible outline for introducing (I) and reinforcing (R) the research levels can be suggested.

GRADE LEVELS

		3	4	5	6	7	8	9	10	11	12
T											
A	Fact-finding	I	R	R	R	R	R	R	R	R	R
X	Asking / Searching		I	R	R	R	R	R	R	R	R
O	Examining / Organizing			I	R	R	R	R	R	R	R
N	Evaluating / Deliberating					I	R	R	R	R	R
O	Integrating / Concluding								I	R	R
M	Conceptualizing										I
Y											

Level 1 Research: Fact-finding

At this level of research, students find basic facts using simple locating skills. The students usually begin the project with an overview of the subject supplied by the teacher or the textbook.

Fact-finding is the level of research most often performed. Students start at this level in the third or fourth grade when they first look up facts in the library. At that age, students are excited by mastering the necessary locating skills. Later, the appeal of this level of research must come from interest in the research subject.

Library media specialists can use fact-finding research as a library orientation unit for first-year students. Instead of marching students through a tour, library media specialists can teach skills of locating by having students explore the library to find tidbits of information about a relevant subject. English classes studying American literature can find facts about life in America during the time periods being studied. The students' facts can be collected into a quiz bowl or trivia game that can be played in the classroom. Students discover interesting information and become familiar with the library without the deadly tour.

Fact-finding research can be valuable for many grade levels and classes, but it should not be the only one ever assigned. If students are to develop thoughtful research skills, teachers and library media specialists must consciously plan assignments at higher levels of the taxonomy.

Level 2 Research: Asking / Searching

At this second level of the taxonomy, students define the specific problem they want to pursue by asking questions to be answered with their research. Students use various research strategies, including a research process, to find the answers.

The asking / searching level of the taxonomy involves the students in thinking about their topics. Because students begin with questions to answer or a problem to solve, they become personally involved in their research.

Library media specialists teach research strategies like use of subject headings, browsing for regular and reference books, and use of a research process.

Research in elementary school should progress to this second level after a couple of introductory, fact-finding units.

A successful research unit at this level might involve whole-class participation in writing appropriate questions. A fourth-grade class studying different countries of the world can choose general research questions which each student uses in researching a particular country:

1. Where is the country located?

2. What is the climate like?

3. What do people wear?

4. What are the most popular foods?

5. What do the people do for entertainment or recreation?

Asking / searching research will be appropriate for many units on the high school level also. A biology class can gather basic information about animals in a "Name that Animal" unit (developed by the biology teachers at Fayetteville High School, Fayetteville, Arkansas). The students each have an animal to investigate by finding answers to questions generated by the teacher or the class:

1. What is the scientific taxonomy of the animal (phylum, order, class, family, genus, species)?

2. What are the characteristics of the phylum?

3. What is the habitat of the animal?

4. What are the morphological characteristics?

5. What is the geographical distribution?

6. What animals are close relatives (at least in the same family)?

Level 3 Research: Examining / Organizing

By the end of elementary school, students may be ready for the third level of the research taxonomy. At this level, students write higher level questions ("why" and "how," not just "who," "what," "when," and "where") and decide whether or not the information they have found answers their questions. In addition, students categorize and organize their information.

This level of research is the highest level appropriate for most elementary students. It is also well suited to many high school units. As an important part of this level, students learn to organize information. This skill is essential for students to learn in elementary or junior high school and to practice in high school. Students should not proceed to higher levels of the research taxonomy until they are able to organize the information they find.

Skills at this level fit well into a biographical research unit. Each student picks a famous person within the guidelines set up by the teacher/library media specialist (famous people in American history, in fashion, in mathematics). The students write their own questions, making sure that some of the questions are high level ("why?" or "how?"). After finding answers to the questions, the students categorize and organize their information. If they choose to organize chronologically, their categories will be based on dates; if they organize topically, their categories will be subjects like training, problems encountered, accomplishments, influence on history.

Level 4 Research: Evaluating / Deliberating

Students in junior high school and above should be given practice in evaluating material and ideas. Junior high students will evaluate according to criteria set up by the library media specialist or classroom teacher. As the students develop skills in evaluation, they can learn to set their own criteria. High-level evaluation (recognizing deceptive arguments, detecting bias) will not be introduced until senior high school.

The students at this level of research do more than evaluate each piece of information. They must also be open to all sides of an issue and be willing to think about the evidence as a whole. Careful attention should be paid to the developmental level of the students before level 4 research is assigned. Young or immature students will have difficulty seeing both sides of an issue.

At level 4, students present arguments for both sides of an issue (as they might do in a panel discussion) or argue one side (by participating in a debate). Students may also highlight the best conclusion that they find and argue its acceptance, but they are not expected to create their own conclusion. Junior high may be the ideal time to introduce this level of research—at what age do students love to argue and question more than the junior high years?

Junior high students, who might be debating the desirability of electing our president by popular vote rather than with the electoral college, might use the following evaluation criteria for their information:

1. Is this piece of information a fact or an opinion?

2. Is this information accurate (compared to information in other sources)?

3. Is this information important or unimportant?

Senior high students, who are studying a multifaceted topic such as South African apartheid, would have to expand evaluation criteria to include bias, fallacies of reasoning, and point of view.

Level 5 Research: Integrating / Concluding

At this level of research, students will be integrating the information they have gathered with what they already know, thus putting the new information into a personal context. The students will draw their own conclusions based on the information found.

Students must be clear about their main point, represented by the thesis statement, and must be able to support that point with evidence from their research. Examples of successful thesis statements at this level of research include the following:

> In recent years America's role in the tiny country of El Salvador has prompted much comparison to the part it played in the early stages of Vietnam. The validity of this analogy and its possible effect upon U.S. foreign policy is an important topic and one warranting serious consideration.   — William Reid Kincaid

> Mass media, especially television, have had a profound effect on the way Americans form opinions. A small segment of the population has near control over our election system, and that is not what the shapers of our government had in mind.   — Jamie Smith

> China and the Soviet Union are in conflict, not only for physical reasons, but also because of the changing ideological positions of the two governments.
>   — Theodore Philip Bashor

(Theses taken from papers submitted to Ms. Judy Gregson, Fayetteville High School.)

Most research units at level 5 will involve some teaching by the library media specialist of sophisticated research skills such as the evaluation of sources, the use of primary sources, or the development of conclusions from evidence located.

Ideally, most high school students should attempt research at the integrating / concluding level before they graduate.

Level 6 Research: Conceptualizing

The conceptualizing level is the highest level of research. In it, students form their own concepts, models, or theories based on the evidence collected, evaluated, and integrated. This level of research will be reached by few high school students and not even by all college students. Advanced high school students can be given the opportunity to perform individual research at this level; other high school students can be given the experience with group work. After each member of the group has completed library research, members can brainstorm together concepts or programs based on their research.

Practical, community-minded problem solving (designing a program to reduce litter or to alleviate teenage drinking and driving) is appropriate for high school research at the conceptualizing level.

Students identify the problem, conduct the research in the library and the community, and evaluate the effectiveness of programs already in place.

Given that base of library and community research, students propose a program that improves on or replaces the programs already in place. Students describe the new program in detail and justify its potential effectiveness.

By directing students toward problem solving rather than theoretical research, library media specialists and teachers can give students successful experience at the conceptualizing level. Students who can convince the school or community to put their concepts into practice will be rewarded by seeing the positive outcome of their research and its impact on others.

THE RESEARCH TAXONOMY AT A GLANCE

The research taxonomy is divided into six levels, but these are not completely separate from each other. The thinking skills involved in each level build upon those used in the previous levels, so that library research becomes a continuum of thinking skills. The essential characteristic of each level can be identified, however, which may help teachers and library media specialists work easily with the research taxonomy in planning library research units.

Key Characteristics of Research Taxonomy Levels

Level	*Characteristic*
1. Fact-finding	Finding simple facts
2. Asking / Searching	Finding answers to questions
3. Examining / Organizing	Reorganizing information
4. Evaluating / Deliberating	Evaluating information and conclusions
5. Integrating / Concluding	Drawing conclusions
6. Conceptualizing	Creating original solutions

Leading students to research at high levels of the taxonomy will help them develop skills to become independent researchers and thoughtful users of information. Teaching library research as a thinking process has the same goal as the one identified by Raymond Nickerson for teaching thinking: "And our hope must be that students will learn far more than we yet know how to teach" (Nickerson, 1987, p. 37).

Chapter 2

THOUGHTFUL REACTIONS
TO RESEARCH

Jason slammed his books on the library table. Everyone's eyes blinked at the unexpected explosion.

"I can't believe Mrs. Johnson!" The bitter edge to Jason's voice threatened to erupt into a tirade. His three friends at the table listened eagerly; they also were taking American history from Mrs. Johnson.

"She just handed back my research paper with a 'D' on it. Listen to what she wrote on the paper."

Jason pulled his glasses to the end of his nose and mimicked Mrs. Johnson in a nasal tone. " 'You seem to have found some interesting information, but I had a hard time following what you were trying to say. Your paper could have used better organization, more thought, and much more creativity. I felt like I was reading excerpts from the encyclopedia at times.' Where did she think I got most of the information—of course it sounded like the encyclopedia!"

Eugene spoke up. "Yeah, I got a lousy grade, too. When I was writing my paper, I was so bored I kept falling asleep. I kind of liked my subject, though—the Rosenbergs, those people who were executed for spying."

Louis was the wise one. "Anytime you write a research paper, it's boring. You'd think teachers would learn better after awhile and stop assigning research. I figure the teachers get what they deserve."

Louis's assessment of the situation was wrong; it was not the *research* that was boring. Instead, the problem lay with the assigned *reaction* to the research. Teachers who design assignments to lift students above the copy-from-the-encyclopedia level of research must just as carefully plan the second phase of the assignment—the student's product.

For every research assignment, students must create a product. Unless they use the knowledge gained from their research, that knowledge becomes inert, dead. Mrs. Johnson could have rescued her students from the traditional copy-from-the-encyclopedia syndrome by encouraging them to produce a product in which they thought about their research material and reacted to it rather than merely copied or paraphrased it.

Although scholarly, written term papers are appropriate research reactions (especially for students who will be going to college), teachers should not feel that term papers are the *only* possible culminating activity. A myriad of creative possibilities exist, and these alternatives often spark interest in even the most bored students, leading them to new levels of involvement in research. Involved students are *thinking* students.

The level of thought in students' reactions to research may vary from simple to complex; these levels can be displayed in a taxonomy comparable to the taxonomy of thought levels for research presented in chapter 1. The reaction level chosen for each research project will depend on the objectives of the teacher and library media specialist.

TAXONOMY OF THOUGHTFUL REACTIONS (REACTS)*

Recalling

Explaining

Analyzing

Challenging

Transforming

Synthesizing

Level 1 Reaction: Recalling

Students at this level simply recall and report the main facts discovered through the research; they do not analyze or restructure the information.

Level 2 Reaction: Explaining

This level involves restating, summarizing, or paraphrasing information. The students give examples, explain events or actions, and understand the information well enough to put it in a new context.

Level 3 Reaction: Analyzing

Students show the information categories and relationships (causes, effects, problems, solutions) discovered during research. They may compare one part of the subject with another or place the subject in another time or place and predict what will change.

---

*Adapted from "The Three Rs of School Libraries" by Barbara Stripling, *Arkansas Libraries* 42, no. 1 (March 1985): 20-24. Reprinted with permission, Arkansas Library Association.

Level 4 Reaction: Challenging

Students communicate critical judgments about their subject based on internal or external standards. The students may use their own standards or those decided upon by the class or teacher. They may judge a subject based on its own merit or compared to similar subjects. Students do not react with "I don't believe it" or "I didn't like it," although they may start with those personal reactions to build their judgments.

Level 5 Reaction: Transforming

Students at the transforming level integrate more than one piece of information, form their own conclusions, and present their conclusions in a creative format. Students find this level of reactions the most enjoyable and especially like producing group reactions based on individual research and group conclusions.

Level 6 Reaction: Synthesizing

At the synthesizing level, students create new concepts or programs based on their research. Students must visualize or verbalize their new concepts effectively. Sixth-level reactions are often delivered to audiences outside the school, such as community or service groups.

CREATIVE ALTERNATIVES TO RESEARCH PAPERS

Mrs. Johnson might have gone further in her planning than deciding the thought level she wanted. She could have assigned a *creative* reaction as an alternative to the traditional research paper. Asking the students to re-try Julius and Ethel Rosenberg might have inspired even the jaded Louis to think about the research in an analytical and creative way.

The suggested assignments which follow each step of the taxonomy below offer teachers and library media specialists alternatives to traditional "term papers" or "reports." Students are asked to "react" to their research in a new way. Since the assignments are generic, they can be adapted to most subject areas.

Also listed for each level of the taxonomy are verbs to be used as idea starters for additional reaction assignments at each thought level.

Every time students choose a visual or oral reaction, they must also produce a brief, written explanation of the project and a list of sources used for the research. The written explanation will allow students to show and teachers to evaluate the thought behind the project.

The levels of the research taxonomy and the REACTS taxonomy are correlated. If students have researched at level 1 / fact-finding, they probably will react at level 1 / recalling. Exceptions to the level 1 / level 1 match should be made only with justification by the teacher and/or library media specialist.

The Research Taxonomy	*The REACTS Taxonomy*
Fact-finding	Recalling
Asking / Searching	Explaining
Examining / Organizing	Analyzing
Evaluating / Deliberating	Challenging
Integrating / Concluding	Transforming
Conceptualizing	Synthesizing

Recalling (Fact-finding Research) — Level 1

Verbs: arrange; cluster; define; find; identify; label; list; locate; match; name; recall; recount; repeat; reproduce; select; sort; state.

Example Assignments

1. Arrange words important to your research in a crossword puzzle.

2. Select information discovered in your research and portray it on a poster/collage.

3. Write a letter to a friend recalling the information you gathered.

4. Reproduce the information you researched in a simplified format for inclusion in a third-grade reading book.

5. Based on your research, state five questions a television reporter might ask if he/she were preparing a feature news story on your subject. Answer the questions.

A level 1 research assignment combined with a level 1 reaction might follow the pattern below:

Sample Assignment: Math

Students will:

Research —
 — be given a list of famous mathematicians.
 — use specific reference books selected by the library media specialist to discover each mathematician's major contribution.

Reaction —
 — use the researched information as definitions and answers for a *crossword puzzle*.

Explaining (Asking / Searching Research)—Level 2

Verbs: apply; cite; complete; convert; demonstrate; describe; document; dramatize; emulate; estimate; expand; explain; expound; express; generalize; give example; illustrate; imagine; paraphrase; portray; prepare; present; produce; propose; restate; review; search; show; solve; speculate; summarize; support; survey; translate; use.

Example Assignments

1. Dramatize a particularly exciting event associated with your research in an on-the-spot report.

2. Illustrate important features about your research in a mobile.

3. Write and present a "You Are There" news program about a particular event or person you researched.

4. Keep a journal in which you present your reactions, thoughts, and feelings about your research.

5. Show the events of your research on a map and explain the importance of each event.

6. Complete each of the following statements based on your research: My research made me wish that ...; realize that ...; decide that ...; wonder about ...; see that ...; believe that ...; feel that ...; hope that....

7. Cut out newspaper ads that would have interested a historical figure you have researched. Explain their importance to the historical figure.

8. Demonstrate the character and personality of a historical person by filling a paper bag with modern objects that reveal the major facets to the person's character.

9. Prepare a job application or resume for a person you have researched.

10. Imagine you are an eighteenth-century student. As such, review the information you have discovered in your research and react to it.

11. Propose a party with three celebrities invited to honor the person you have researched. Describe the menu and activities. Justify your choices.

12. Become a person in the historical era you have researched; write a letter to someone describing a specific event, problem, invention, or fad.

A level 2 research and reaction assignment might be:

Sample Assignment: History

Students will:

Research—
   —be assigned a specific historical event.
   —write questions about the main points they want to research.
   —use a research process to find information about their event in one reference book and one regular book.

Reaction—
   —dramatize the information in the form of an *on-the-spot radio report* such as the famous Hindenburg crash description. Incorporate background information about the topic into the dramatization.

Analyzing (Examining / Organizing Research)—Level 3

Verbs: analyze; apply; arrange; associate; break down; categorize; change; characterize; classify; compare; compile; construct; contrast; correlate; diagram; differentiate; discover; discriminate; dissect; distinguish; divide; examine; experiment; extend; group; infer; interpret; manipulate; map; modify; organize; outline; plan; question; relate; revise; rewrite; scrutinize; select; separate; sequence; sift; simplify; solve; transplant; uncover; utilize; verify.

Example Assignments

1. Create a time line for the events which led up to the situation you researched. Correlate social, political, religious, educational, and technological events.

2. Transplant an event or famous person from one time period, country, or ecological system to another time or place. Explain the changes that would occur.

3. Construct a collage examining the social pressures influencing your subject.

4. Characterize your researched historical person in an obituary which makes clear his/her role in the conflicts of the day.

5. Reconstruct the personality and career of a person you have researched and play the role of that person in a "What's My Line" game.

6. Cast a film version of the event you researched. The characters could be represented by actors working today or classmates. Explain your choices carefully.

7. Compare your lifestyle and neighborhood to those of people living in the time you have researched.

8. Write a letter to the editor scrutinizing a local issue. Support your opinions with specific details from your research.

9. Rewrite a historical event from two different points of view.

Sample Assignment: Health

Students will:

Research—
—choose a specific communicable disease (for example, polio) to research.
—write questions that will lead to finding out about the history of the disease and important social and political events around the time a cure/vaccine for the disease was discovered.
—use a research process to find information about the topic in reference and regular books and periodicals if appropriate.
—categorize every item of information by the question it answers and by the time or year in which it occurred.

Reaction—
—construct a *time line* to correlate the medical research to social and political events.

Challenging (Evaluating / Deliberating Research)—Level 4

Verbs: appraise; argue; assess; compare; criticize; debate; defend; determine; discriminate; evaluate; grade; investigate; judge; justify; modify; prioritize; rank; rate; refute; review; support; value; weigh.

Example Assignments

1. Produce a critical review (of a book, movie, or play) which can be printed in a local newspaper or aired on local television or radio stations.

2. Act as an attorney and argue to convict or acquit a historical character or a country for a crime or misdeed.

3. Determine as a movie producer whether or not to make a film of an actual historical event, with justification for the decision.

4. Defend your judgment that a research subject (if it is an invention, machine, or some other item) should be placed in a time capsule to be dug up in 100 years.

5. Justify the punishment or nonpunishment of a historical villain.

6. Judge the merits of a researched subject by conducting a mock trial.

7. Debate the issues of a controversial research topic with a classmate who researched the same topic.

8. Evaluate your library's collection of information on your topic. Write a letter to the library media specialist requesting additional materials on specific aspects of the topic. Justify your opinion.

A challenging reaction combined with evaluating / deliberating research assignment might include:

Sample Assignment: English

Students will:

Research—
   —read a novel published since 1940.
   —use a research process to find critical information about the author and novel.
   —assess the quality of the novel according to standards established in class and judge the quality of the criticisms found in reviews of the novel.
   —combine their own critical opinions with those of the critics they judge to be most reputable.

Reaction—
   —produce one of the following:
      —a *book review* for the school or local newspaper.
      —a videotaped review for local public access television or for viewing by other English classes.
      —an audiotaped review in the style of those aired on National Public Radio for playback on the local radio station or to English classes.

Transforming (Integrating / Concluding Research)—Level 5

Verbs: blend; build; combine; compile; compose; conclude; construct; convince; create; decide; design; develop; forecast; formulate; generate; imagine; modify; persuade; plan; predict; produce; propose; revise; speculate; structure.

Example Assignments

   1. Design and produce a television commercial or a whole advertising campaign which presents your research results to the class.

   2. Create a board game that incorporates the major conclusions you reached about your researched subject.

   3. Write a poem or short story that expresses your new knowledge or insight.

   4. Dramatize a famous historical event. The dramatization should make clear your interpretation of the event.

   5. Predict your reaction to your research subject as a resident of the future.

   6. Compose a speech that a historical person might deliver about a present-day national issue.

A level 5 research and reaction assignment might be:

Sample Assignment: Science

Students will:

Research—
- — choose an ecological problem facing our country such as smog, acid rain, litter, or chemical waste dumps.
- — use a research process to investigate and evaluate that problem and solutions that have been tried.
- — draw conclusions about the best solution to the problem and be able to support those conclusions with evidence.

Reaction—
- — use the researched information and conclusions to design and produce an *advertising campaign* to convince viewers and readers to act on the "best solution" proposed by the researcher. The campaign could include a brochure, television commercial, bumper sticker, etc.

Synthesizing (Conceptualizing Research)—Level 6

Verbs: build a model program; create; design; develop; devise; generate; hypothesize; invent; propose; theorize.

Example Assignments

1. Develop a model program to address a social problem that you have researched.

2. Invent a new animal; explain its effect on other animals and on the environment.

3. Create a new country and hypothesize about the change in the balance of power in the world.

4. Design a new building, machine, process, experiment based on theories developed from your research.

5. Develop proposed legislation to address national, state, or local issues.

6. Devise an ethical code for present-day researchers or scientists which could regulate their activities in a particular field.

The highest level research and reaction might produce an assignment like the following:

Sample Assignment: Psychology/Sociology

Students will:

Research—
- — use a research process to investigate an adolescent problem (drinking, suicide, crime, dropouts).

—investigate community programs that treat or attempt to alleviate that problem.

—evaluate the extent of the adolescent problem and the successes and failures of the community programs.

—design a *model program* to be instituted in the school, community, or church which would address the adolescent problem in a new way or would improve the services offered by the community programs already in place.

Reaction—

—generate a presentation on the model program to be delivered to the appropriate agencies. Include visuals and handouts with the presentation.

BENEFITS OF REACTS ASSIGNMENTS

Besides the obvious advantage of making research more meaningful and enjoyable for students, the REACTS assignments offer other benefits as well. Because many of the assignments are not written, they allow learning disabled students to bypass their disabilities while creating their research reactions. In addition, many of the assignments can be group projects which allow students to brainstorm together and capitalize on the strengths of other students.

A further benefit of the REACTS assignments is that they help teachers match the assigned research reactions with the ability levels of the students. Since assignments can be created at each level of the taxonomy for the same research unit, teachers can assign a recalling reaction to a struggling student but require an analyzing reaction from a student with greater ability. The following presents assignments at every level of the taxonomy for a research unit on Ancient Greece.

Sample Assignments for Ancient Greece on REACTS Taxonomic Levels

Objective: Students will gain an understanding of culture, customs, and lifestyle in Ancient Greece.

Level 1—Recalling
Write a letter to a friend describing the information you discovered about your assigned topic.

Level 2—Explaining
Interview ordinary Greek people (soldier, slave, statesman, young woman) about their daily life.

Level 3—Analyzing
Pick a famous Greek and explain the adaptations that person would have to make to live in American society today. Show what the historic person would do and would buy today.

Level 4—Challenging
Select a famous Greek soldier or statesman and write a recommendation for him to receive (or not receive) the *Time* magazine "Man of the Year" designation. In order to receive the honor, the person must have had a profound impact on the world situation.

Level 5—Transforming
Research specific aspects of Ancient Greece and create a television program entitled "Good Morning, Greece" which would include interviews, on-the-spot reports, news items, feature stories, theatre reviews, advertisements, and other segments.

Level 6—Synthesizing

Based on your research about the decline of the ancient Greek civilization, develop a model for the decline of any civilization and suggestions for civilizations wishing to prevent decline.

Another benefit from using REACTS is that teachers can devise assignments that appeal to all learning styles. Students can complete written, oral, visual, or dramatic presentations based on their research.

The most exciting aspect of REACTS assignments is that students enjoy them and willingly learn the information from their own research as well as the information communicated by other presenters. Given the promise of a creative product, students discover that neither researching nor reacting to research is painful, boring, or otherwise connected to the copy-from-the-encyclopedia research project that exasperates Jason, bores Eugene, and embitters Louis.

Chapter 3

THE RESEARCH
PROCESS

"Mrs. Weaver, I'm having trouble with my health research report." Sarah's brow furrowed in misery.

"What is your subject, Sarah?" the library media specialist asked sympathetically.

"My topic is death and dying in Asia. So I found the books on 'Asia,' but they were all about history. So I looked in an encyclopedia, but all I found under 'Asia' was the 'Asiatic flu.' I took notes on that, but I don't think they're right. And, like, I don't know where else to look. The paper is due day after tomorrow."

"Sarah, do you have an assignment sheet I could look at?"

"No, Mr. Beachum didn't give us one, but I know we're supposed to have three sources. It's just that I can't find three sources on death and dying in Asia."

"Was your topic 'Euthanasia?' " Mrs. Weaver asked to confirm her suspicions.

"Yeah, that was it! 'Youth in Asia.' "

Mrs. Weaver smiled. "You're in luck, Sarah. I can help you find three sources on 'Euthanasia' quickly. But you'll have to work hard to take notes on them by tomorrow. Maybe I can help you write some research questions that will help you focus. Let's start with a definition and overview in the encyclopedia...."

Sarah's forehead smoothed as she followed Mrs. Weaver to the reference collection.

Sarah's scattershot approach led her to leap into the middle of her research with little understanding of what her topic was or where to look for information. Without a process to guide her thinking about the research, she could not complete the assignment successfully.

Most students do not automatically think during research. If teachers and library media specialists accept the importance of students' *thinking* during research, then they must also accept the responsibility for teaching thinking skills.

Teaching students to think about research involves giving them a thinking frame, "a guide to organizing and supporting thought processes" (Perkins, 1987, p. 47). The thinking frame for research (which serves as a guide for *how* to think rather than for *what* to think) is the *research process*.

OVERVIEW OF THE PROCESS

The ten-step research process presented in this book can be used by students of any age for any library research. Each step of the process includes specific study and thinking skills as well as teaching and learning strategies.

At critical points in the process, *reflection points* direct students to evaluate the work they have just completed. If problems are apparent, students revise or re-perform the previous research-process step until they are able to answer the reflection-point questions satisfactorily.

An overview of the research process is listed below:

Step 1: Choose a broad topic.

Step 2: Get an overview of the topic.

Step 3: Narrow the topic.
Reflection Point: Is my topic a good one?

Step 4: Develop a thesis or statement of purpose.
Reflection Point: Does my thesis or statement of purpose represent an effective, overall concept for my research?

Step 5: Formulate questions to guide research.
Reflection Point: Do the questions provide a foundation for my research?

Step 6: Plan for research and production.
Reflection Point: Is the research / production plan workable?

Step 7: Find / Analyze / Evaluate sources.
Reflection Point: Are my sources usable and adequate?

Step 8: Evaluate evidence / Take notes / Compile bibliography.
Reflection Point: Is my research complete?

Step 9: Establish conclusions / Organize information into an outline.
Reflection Point: Are my conclusions based on researched evidence?
Does my outline logically organize conclusions and evidence?

Step 10: Create and present final product.
Reflection Point: Is my paper / project satisfactory?

TEACHING THE RESEARCH PROCESS

The Research Process as a Thinking Frame

To learn any thinking frame (like the research process), learners must acquire it first through direct instruction. The research process must be taught by teachers and library media specialists in conjunction with curricular research units.

The second stage in acquiring a thinking frame is practice until its use becomes automatic. Students should be made aware they are practicing a research process every time they perform library research. If an entire school district uses the same process, students will receive consistent practice throughout their school years, and no library media specialist or teacher will have to teach the entire process at one time.

The final stage in acquisition of a thinking frame is transfer to other situations. If students use the process any time they need information, whether for a class project or for their own interest, they have learned an effective thinking frame for research—the research process (Perkins, 1987).

The Research Process and the Taxonomies

Although every step of the research process is essential, it is not essential that *students* perform each step on every assignment. Depending on teacher objectives, student abilities, and research level, some steps may be compensated for by the teacher or library media specialist.

The level of research is more important than the grade level in determining the steps of the process to be performed by students. If twelfth graders are doing simple, fact-finding research, they will perform few steps, despite their ability to do them all.

Teachers and library media specialists can plan who will be responsible for each step of the research process. Although many variations are possible, plans for each taxonomic level are suggested below. Some steps will be performed by the students (S), some by the teacher (T), and some by the library media specialist (LMS).

Grade 3: Fact-finding research / Recalling reaction

(FIRST LEVEL)

Each student selects a bird by random drawing, researches it in the library, and then presents the information on a poster.

T	Step 1 (Broad Topic): Assigned by the teacher.
T	Step 2 (Overview): Offered by the teacher in class.
T	Step 3 (Narrow Topic): Assigned by random drawing.
T + S	Step 4 (Statement of Purpose): Written by the class together; identical for all students.
T + S	Step 5 (Questions): Written by the class together; general questions identical for all students.
T	Step 6 (Research/Production Plan): Organized by the teacher.
LMS	Step 7 (Find Sources): Library media specialist has pulled the sources for the class.
S	Step 8 (Take Notes): Students take notes to answer their questions.
T + S	Step 9 (Outline): Written by class together; students insert their own information into the general outline.
LMS + S	Step 10 (Prepare Presentation): Library media specialist helps with creating the posters.

Grade 4: Asking / Searching research / Explaining reaction

(SECOND LEVEL)

Students pick a country and research the customs in that country using two sources. As their reaction, they fill a paper bag with three or four objects or pictures that represent the main customs they found and present these objects to the class while explaining the customs.

T	Step 1 (Broad Topic): Assigned by the teacher.
T + S	Step 2 (Overview): Offered by the teacher and discussed in class (What are customs?).
S	Step 3 (Narrow Topic): Countries selected by the students.
T + S	Step 4 (Statement of Purpose): Written by the class together; identical for all students.
S	Step 5 (Questions): Students write research questions after instruction by teacher or library media specialist.
T	Step 6 (Research/Production Plan): Organized by the teacher.
LMS + S	Step 7 (Find Sources): Library media specialist works with students on subject headings and suggested Dewey areas; students find two books each.
S	Step 8 (Take Notes): Students take notes to answer their questions.
T + S	Step 9 (Outline): Written by the class together; students insert their own information into the general outline.
S	Step 10 (Prepare Presentation): Students find their objects or pictures; prepare their oral presentations from their outlines.

Grades 5-6: Examining / Organizing research / Analyzing reaction

(THIRD LEVEL)

Students each pick one dinosaur, research it, and then project the effect on the countryside, the people, the cities, and the economy if their dinosaur came back to life. They portray their information in either written or visual format.

T	Step 1 (Broad Topic): Assigned by the teacher.
T + S	Step 2 (Overview): General information about dinosaurs is discussed in class; students read overviews about dinosaurs to help them pick one to research.
S	Step 3 (Narrow Topic): Students pick their own dinosaurs to research.
S	Step 4 (Statement of Purpose): Students write their own statements of purpose after instruction by the teacher.
S	Step 5 (Questions): Students write their own research questions after instruction by the teacher.
T + S	Step 6 (Research/Production Plan): Teacher offers a choice of formats; students pick the one they think will work best for their dinosaur and use a teacher-developed worksheet to plan research and production.

S + LMS   Step 7 (Find/Analyze Sources): Students find their own sources and look carefully at them to be sure they use the most appropriate ones; library media specialist teaches some analysis skills.

S   Step 8 (Take Notes): Students take notes to answer their questions.

S   Step 9 (Outline): Students organize their own information after instruction by the teacher.

S   Step 10 (Prepare Presentation): Students prepare their final projects; the teacher and library media specialist help when needed.

Grade 7: Evaluating / Deliberating research / Challenging reaction

(FOURTH LEVEL)

Each student in a life science class picks a disease and researches it. Students then debate in groups of four about which disease should receive the most governmental and scientific funding (to find cure, to carry out mass inoculations, to offer aid to victims of the disease). Historical diseases are treated as if they were in existence today.

T   Step 1 (Broad Topic): Assigned by the teacher.

T   Step 2 (Overview): Overview of the impact of disease on society and of the progression of diseases through history is offered in class.

S   Step 3 (Narrow Topic): Students choose a specific disease.

S   Step 4 (Thesis Statement): Students write thesis statement for their debate based on instruction by teacher.

T + S   Step 5 (Questions): Students write questions based on instruction by teacher and class discussion; questions for each student will be very similar.

T   Step 6 (Research/Production Plan): Organized by the teacher.

S + LMS   Step 7 (Find / Analyze / Evaluate Sources): Students find sources, analyze them according to their usefulness, and evaluate them according to criteria set up by the teacher or library media specialist; instruction by library media specialist is essential.

S + LMS   Step 8 (Evaluate Evidence / Take Notes): Students evaluate each piece of evidence before taking notes based around their research questions; instruction by library media specialist is probably essential.

T + S   Step 9 (Outline): Students follow the general outline written in class, inserting their own evidence.

S   Step 10 (Prepare Presentation): General rules for debate are given by the teacher; students debate in groups of four.

Grade 10: Integrating / Concluding research / Transforming reaction

(FIFTH LEVEL)

For an American history class, students find out how a twentieth-century invention (for example, the telephone) was developed and how it changed America. Then they invent something similar (for example, an ESP phone) and predict how it would transform America. They design an ad campaign to present their information and conclusions.

At this taxonomic level of research, the students perform almost every step of the research process. In this assignment, the broad topic (step 1) and the research / production plan (step 6) have been assigned by the teacher. The library media specialist teaches analysis and evaluation skills at steps 7 and 8 and any other skills that seem difficult for students. The major new skill added at this level is establishing conclusions at step 9, and students will need instruction for this.

Grade 12: Conceptualizing research / Synthesizing reaction

(SIXTH LEVEL)

Students in a health class investigate the environmental, physical, and psychological aspects of wellness. They evaluate the evidence they gather and draw their own conclusions about the major wellness factors, deciding which can be manipulated to improve a person's well-being. Based on their conclusions, students devise a wellness test. Working with local firms, they administer the test to employees and design individual health-improvement plans. The students use compiled results to develop company programs that will help employees fulfill their individual wellness plans (adapted from a project developed by Dr. Tom Williams, Fayetteville High School).

Students at this level of research often perform every step of the research process. In most cases, students at this level will need instruction in advanced search strategies and evaluation techniques from the library media specialist in order to perform in-depth research.

THE PARTNERSHIP BETWEEN TEACHERS AND LIBRARY MEDIA SPECIALISTS

Library media specialists and teachers have a symbiotic relationship. Teaching students a research process isolated from the curriculum is useless. Similarly, requiring students to perform research without teaching a research process frustrates the students and produces unsuccessful projects. The library media specialist is the process specialist; the teacher is the content specialist. Both process and content are necessary for a successful research experience.

The teacher/library-media-specialist team-teaching experience can be rewarding if a few simple procedures are followed and if an atmosphere of mutual respect exists.

Step One: Brainstorming Session

At the initial session, the teacher and library media specialist can brainstorm exciting alternatives for the unit being planned. The teacher brings to the meeting the content objectives, an idea of the time to be spent on the unit, and a knowledge of the students' abilities and learning styles. The library media specialist brings a knowledge of the students' previous library training and of the library skills objectives to be incorporated. The library media specialist should have available copies of the research taxonomy, the REACTS taxonomy, and the research process.

Using the content and process objectives and the time line, the teacher and library media specialist determine the levels of research and reaction. One- or two-day units should be limited to the lower levels of research and reaction.

After the levels have been established, the teacher and library media specialist brainstorm about the final product. By using the lists of verbs and the generic assignments in chapter 2, the teaching team can generate several alternative assignments in minutes. One can be chosen at this meeting, or the teacher can reflect upon the brainstormed list and make the choice later.

Step Two: Planning Session

When the teacher is ready to start planning the unit, the library media specialist pulls out a research planning sheet (see handout 3.1). Together they briefly describe the unit and the final product and list the chosen taxonomic levels of research and reaction.

Then they write objectives for both content (subject area) and process (library) skills. These may be listed in terms of teacher objectives, student objectives, or student behavioral objectives.

After the objectives have been established, the teacher and library media specialist decide which steps of the research process will be performed by the students. Then, the teaching team divides the responsibilities for the unit. They decide what each will do before the students arrive in the library media center, who will teach which skills, and who will be responsible for follow-up.

Step Three: Assignment Sheet

After all the plans have been made, the teacher and/or the library media specialist prepare an assignment sheet. It includes the objectives, stated in terms that the students can readily understand; perhaps a schedule with daily goals (especially if the time in the library is long); a description of the final product; information about the presentation of the project; and evaluation criteria. The assignment sheet will give students a structure and focus and will increase their success.

Step Four: Execution of the Unit

When working with students in the library, both the library media specialist and the teacher should model use of the research process and effective thinking. They can suggest alternatives (like possible topics or questions), keep an open mind, respond to student input, ask questions, and search for new ideas. Emerson is often quoted, "What you do speaks so loudly, they can't hear what you say" (Costa, 1985).

The library media specialist and teacher must recognize their different areas of strength. The library media specialist is better at helping students find and evaluate information. The teacher is better at helping students choose information compatible with the classroom studies.

One awkward aspect of team teaching is that all teachers have their own opinions about students' work; those opinions may at times be contradictory. What the teacher thinks is a good topic, the library media specialist may reject, knowing there is not enough information available. Awkward situations can be avoided if each professional initials student work as it is checked so that other professionals involved will know the student has already received advice. Research is not a precise science, and thoughtful discussion may be generated when opinions differ.

Step Five: Evaluation of the Unit

The teacher and/or the library media specialist must evaluate the students' work based on evaluation criteria that were explained to the students at the beginning of the assignment. The teacher can judge the content and the library media specialist can evaluate the production and presentation of the project. The library media specialist should be involved in the evaluation; nothing establishes credibility better than being in charge of the almighty grades.

Evaluating the unit itself is also essential. Notes should be written on the research planning sheet of the most and least effective aspects of the unit as well as suggestions for changes. The sheet and any supporting material (copies of assignment sheet, classroom worksheets, library worksheets) are then filed for referral the next time the unit is taught.

THE ROUTE TO THOUGHTFUL RESEARCH

Few teachers or secondary students would begin a cross-country trip without a map. They know they must have a destination in mind and a general idea of the route they will follow. While a trip may last a few days, work on a research project may last several weeks, and having a route for research is as essential as it is for a trip.

The next nine chapters of this book detail the research process, the road map to successful research. Teachers and library media specialists are invited to study the ten-step process, take from it those ideas which seem most useful, and plan their own trips. Side trips and excursions to new and exciting destinations are encouraged as long as the goal remains the same—well-researched, thoughtful library research projects.

RESEARCH PLANNING SHEET

Teacher: _____ Class: _____

Brief description of unit and final product:

Taxonomic level of research: _____

Taxonomic level of reaction: _____

Objectives:

Content	Process

Responsibilities:

Teacher	Library Media Specialist

Dates of unit:

Evaluation/Comments:

Handout 3.1. Barbara K. Stripling and Judy M. Pitts, *Brainstorms and Blueprints: Teaching Library Research as a Thinking Process* (Englewood, Colo.: Libraries Unlimited, 1988).

Chapter 4

STEP ONE
Choose a Broad Topic

Most of the students hurried from the library's classroom area to the reference collection. They were to locate an overview of their broad topic. A few students who had not yet chosen a topic remained seated, listlessly turning magazine pages or browsing through a book of several thousand research subjects.

The library media specialist and classroom teacher began approaching the students individually, quietly asking questions, hoping to discover an interest area.

"What topics have you considered?" Patty was asked.

"I haven't thought of anything." Patty gazed contentedly at the front cover of her notebook on which twenty-five variations of "Patty Loves Danny" were etched.

"Well, what are you interested in?"

"Nothing."

"Do you have any hobbies?"

"No."

"What do you do in your spare time, after school or in the evenings?"

"Nothing."

Nothing. The answer experienced educators dread because, if a research unit is to succeed, the students must choose subjects which interest them. Whether the research project is process centered (objectives related to the research and writing processes) or content centered (curriculum content objectives added to the research and writing processes), students must find topics to engage their interest.

Two factors cause students to have trouble choosing broad topics that interest them. First, many students are "experience illiterates." Their backgrounds are limited by inexperience; their world view is restricted by "teenage myopia." They are disinterested in everything outside their personal world (like, horrors! academic subjects and current events), and they cannot see any connections between their world and viable research topics.

The second topic-limiting factor is that some students have not yet discovered the joys of seeking information or developing new interests. This attitude of inquiry, this "need to know," is the basis for successful student research.

Teachers and library media specialists must help students discover the "right" topics, those which both interest the students and meet the learning objectives of the assignment. The right topics will help students develop the "right" attitude toward research, an openness to new ideas.

To perform the first step of the research process, students must be able to:

1. Discover an interest in an area of research.

2. Distinguish between topics that are researchable and those that are not.

3. Crystallize their own knowledge and feelings about the subject before starting the research.

As students work through this step, they should develop a list of several broad topics.

DISCOVER AN INTEREST IN AN AREA OF RESEARCH

How can teachers and library media specialists help students discover interests and make connections between those interests and research topics? Put more broadly, how can students' minds be opened to the world? Some students have a spark of curiosity; their enthusiasm flares into a steady interest. Other students' minds seem cold, unwilling to warm to the excitement of research.

One technique to help students kindle interests is *freewriting*. The students pick a subject and write continuously for a given period of time (from five minutes to thirty minutes or longer) without pausing to edit or revise. Students follow the path of their own ideas, changing subjects whenever a new thought occurs. Topics of interest often emerge.

An alternative to freewriting is *directed freewriting*, in which the teacher suggests a general subject. The same rules for fluency apply; students let the writing flow without stopping to evaluate.

By working students through some of the following directed-freewriting activities, teachers and library media specialists can encourage interest in several broad topics.

1. Give each student a magazine (out-of-date issues will be fine). The type of magazine can vary according to the assignment (for example, news magazines for general interest or social studies research projects; science magazines for science research). Each student browses the magazine for five minutes to find a topic of interest (which may be in an advertisement rather than an article) and freewrites for fifteen minutes on that subject or related issues.

2. Hand out or display a list of broad topics. Each student picks a topic and freewrites for fifteen minutes (see handout 4.1).

3. Have the students watch the evening news. The next day, they freewrite for fifteen minutes on some item from the news.

4. After class discussion, teacher lecture, or background reading from a text, students freewrite on one or more aspect(s) of an upcoming unit.

5. Assign students a letter of the alphabet. They browse through that volume of several general encyclopedias to identify potential topics. One idea can lead to another; the "Adolescence" article in the "A" volume may lead students to the "Suicide" article in the "S" volume. After browsing, students freewrite about the topics they discovered (Kelly, 1985).

After each freewriting session, students divide into small groups and read their writings (or selected portions) aloud. Group members react positively to something in each writing (such as a well-expressed idea or an interesting thought). These positive reactions build an atmosphere of trust essential for successful group sharing. After sharing, the writer knows what topics interest others.

Students *can* freewrite without sharing, although they will not be able to gauge the reactions of an audience to their topic. Students should have some experience with group sharing, though, before attempting it on a research unit.

In the past few years, publishing companies have become aware of the students' problems with topic selection. Some sources provide extensive lists of subjects (Lamm, 1984; Powell, 1981) but should be viewed as helpful not prescriptive.

DISTINGUISH RESEARCHABLE TOPICS

Several factors are involved in distinguishing researchable topics. The student must consider the probable availability of resources, whether the subject is manageable, whether the subject could be thoughtfully researched, and whether the student's own emotionalism will interfere with the research.

Are Resources Available?

Students usually cannot predict whether materials might be available on a particular subject in a typical school library. Joe may decide to research the history of roller coasters. He does not realize that his topic is esoteric, that little has been written on it, and that his school library would not have purchased materials on roller coaster history. Joe only knows that he is interested in the subject.

Teachers and library media specialists can deal with esoteric topic choices by simply telling students that the topic is not going to work. Characteristically, students like Joe will react defensively. They fail to realize that the adult wants each student to have a successful research experience and hopes to steer everyone to a researchable topic of interest. Joe may feel he and his topic (to which he has now formed an emotional attachment) are being unjustly attacked.

Teachers and library media specialists can head off students' attachment to a single topic by requiring them to list several potential subjects. These students will not be threatened by their teacher's or library media specialist's advice to abandon a topic because of a lack of materials. They can easily choose another broad topic.

Students will also accept the necessity for topic change more readily when they see a clear relationship between their own areas of interest and researchable topics. This relationship can be demonstrated with a Venn diagram. Students must choose a topic from the shaded area, where interest and researchability overlap.

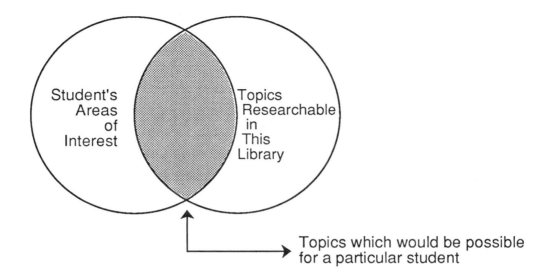

Topics which would be possible
for a particular student

An alternative to having teachers and library media specialists tell students that certain subjects will not work is to let students approach topic selection backwards by assessing the availability of materials before choosing their topics. For this activity, the teacher and library media specialist choose several Dewey ranges that encompass four to five library shelves each. Each Dewey range should include interesting research topics; some shelves may be left out completely. Below is a sample list:

301.3 - 306.8
women, families, teens, terrorism, teen marriage and pregnancy

353.5 - 362.8
FBI, military, warfare, nuclear weapons, Star Wars, drugs, alcohol, child abuse

363 - 381.3
environment, censorship, crime, prisons, education

382 - 398.2
Pony Express, railroads, ships, fashion, holidays, etiquette, folklore

600 - 613.2
inventions, body, medicine, health, diet

613.6 - 621.38
drugs, tobacco, stress, heart, alcohol, psychology, sexually transmitted diseases, pregnancy, electronics

621.381 - 630
solar energy, nuclear power, weapons, airplanes, rockets, ballooning, cars, space technology

770 - 791.43
photography, music, games, circuses, film

796 - 799.3
sports

951 - 972.93
China, Middle East, Vietnam, Africa, Egypt, North American Indians, Aztecs

973.92 - 979.5
American history 1950s-present, state-related information, the West

To begin the activity, each student (or group) draws an assignment sheet with a Dewey range (but not the subjects) written on it (see handout 4.2). Each student or group finds three topics which appear in two sources each. Students look for chapters and continuous pages, not necessarily for whole books on the topics.

Similarly, students can browse *Readers' Guide* issues (including the latest discarded ones), looking for topics that each have two articles listed in magazines the library has available (see handout 4.3).

The students' topics can be compiled and distributed to all class members who may pick one listed or use the list as an idea starter. Inclusion of a topic on a student-generated list does not guarantee adequate research materials, but it does indicate that some sources are available. The teacher reserves the bibliographic information in case a student cannot locate materials.

Students using these approaches will encounter subjects new to them and will have used the availability of resources as a criterion for topic selection.

When asked to consider the availability of resources before they choose a broad topic, students might benefit from considering some of the following questions during brief, topic-selection conferences with their teacher or library media specialist:

1. If the topic is historical, was it important enough to have influenced other events and thus to be included in history books, or was it merely an isolated, interesting event? (Examples of isolated subjects—Anne Frank, Tokyo Rose.)

2. Is the topic based on facts that can be gathered from several sources, or on popular mythology or theory? (Examples of popular mythology and theory—unicorns, Bermuda Triangle.)

3. Is the topic of lasting interest, and thus likely to be included in sources, or is it a current, fleeting issue? (Examples of fleeting issues—the Atlanta child murders, the discovery of Joseph Mengele's body.)

4. Is the topic of fairly general interest, or is it so specialized that most libraries would not have purchased materials on it? (Example of highly specialized topic—history of roller coasters.)

Is the Subject Manageable?

Some topics are not manageable because the subject matter, while interesting on the surface, quickly becomes too complicated. One high school student may be able to do a creditable job researching nuclear arms; another might be overwhelmed by the subject. Some seventh graders might be able to investigate lasers; others would not understand the material. The classroom teacher works with the library media specialist at this point. The teacher will know the students' abilities; the library media specialist will know the complexity of the materials.

Can the Subject Be Thoughtfully Researched?

Research assignments which require high-level thought processes (such as drawing conclusions, analyzing, or evaluating) can intimidate students. Many students are comfortable performing fact-finding-and-rearranging research; they must be challenged to choose broad topics that lead to thoughtful research.

In general, for thoughtful research, students should choose issues and concepts. Tangible topics (objects, animals, or people) often preclude careful thought because students tend to copy the simple, descriptive information. ("The Model T car was first produced by Henry Ford in 1908."; "Abraham Lincoln was born in a log cabin.") Even tangible topics, however, can become thoughtful if students narrow them to a problem or question and combine the tangible aspect with a concept or issue. Instead of describing the Model T car, students could answer the question: How did the Model T car change American society?

At this stage of the research process, students may not be able to foresee the thought-producing aspects of their subject. The adults must think ahead for the students and help them choose topics appropriate for thoughtful research.

Is the Student Too Emotional about the Topic?

A student cannot be objective and thoughtful about a topic which causes an emotional reaction. In junior high school, students should generally be steered away from research projects on death, love, or religion. (Students can be encouraged to pursue such subjects on their own.) In high school if the class is especially immature, research projects on abortion, religion, or drugs can be ruled out.

Even if students are not personally committed to one side of a controversial issue, they may have trouble researching both sides. In fact, students may not be developmentally ready for such high-level evaluation until the latter years of high school, or even later (Bowen, 1987).

CRYSTALLIZE KNOWLEDGE AND FEELINGS ABOUT THE TOPIC

No matter how the broad subject is chosen, students should crystallize their feelings and knowledge about the subject before they begin research. Directed freewriting is especially useful for this process.

Once a tentative broad topic is chosen, students can freewrite for approximately fifteen minutes on what they know and feel and would like to learn about the subject. At the end of the freewriting, students make two columns on a sheet of paper, labeling one side "Knowledge" and the other "Attitudes," leaving a section at the bottom for "Questions." Working through the freewriting, students pull out the facts they know, discover the feelings they have, and identify their questions.

An alternative to this directed freewriting approach is *clustering*. This activity is quicker than directed freewriting, a distinct advantage with students who correlate time invested with emotional attachment to a topic.

Clustering is a "nonlinear brainstorming process" (Rico, 1983, p. 28). Students put their topic in a circle near the center of a page. They then radiate ideas about the topic from that nucleus, concentrating on three areas: facts, feelings, and questions. Ideas can flow in a free-association mode with no concern about any particular order.

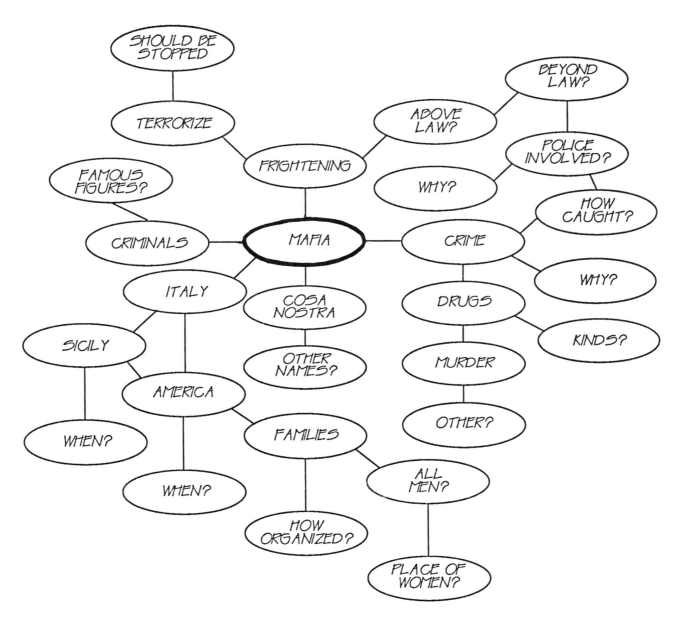

An examination of the end product of either the freewriting or the clustering should help the student and teacher determine the appropriateness of a particular topic for that individual. Students whose feelings far outweigh their knowledge may be too emotional or biased to be rational about their subjects. Students who list no feelings may have no interest in their subject. Students who cannot identify any questions may have chosen a topic with which they are too familiar.

At this stage, students should remain flexible about their topic choice. They may have to change if all the books with information on their topic have been checked out.

COMPENSATION FOR THIS STEP

Selecting a viable research topic is an important skill (especially for students who will continue their education beyond high school), but working through this step requires precious classroom time. If, for whatever reason, the teacher decides that the students do not need to perform this step, it can be completed for them in a variety of ways. For example, students can choose topics from a prepared list. They can arrange in priority order three topics which interest them; assignments can be made on the basis of those selections. Alternately, research subjects can simply be assigned (or drawn from a hat) with no student choice involved. The danger is that students will not develop an interest in their topic and will view the research project as an exercise in rote repetition of information found.

Whatever method is used, this step cannot be skipped entirely. In some way (ideally by student choice), students must begin their research projects with a broad topic clearly in mind.

DIRECTED FREEWRITING TOPICS

Newspapers	Books
Dreams	Hypnosis
Suicide	Women
Families	Jobs
Marriage	Race Relations
Slavery	Crime
Television	School
Fashion	Animals/Pets
Gardening	Diseases
Doctors/Hospitals	Health
Diets	Driving
Advertising	Photography
Music	Movies
Sports	Travel
War	Ecology
Elderly	Pesticides
Military Draft	Sibling Rivalry
Genetic Engineering	Stereotypes
Inventions	Artificial Hearts
Illiteracy	Tobacco
ATVs	Beauty Contests
ESP	Student Rights
Pollution	Nonverbal Communication
Censorship	Divorce
Endangered Species	Soap Operas
Terrorism	Malnutrition
Fads	Computer Crime
Adoption	Parental Kidnapping

Handout 4.1. Barbara K. Stripling and Judy M. Pitts, *Brainstorms and Blueprints: Teaching Library Research as a Thinking Process* (Englewood, Colo.: Libraries Unlimited, 1988).

BROWSING FOR TOPICS / BOOKS

Names of Group Members:

Period: _____

Your Dewey Decimal Area: _____

Directions: Look over the titles, tables of contents, and indexes of the books on your assigned shelves. Find three topics which you think someone might like to research. List two books which contain information on each subject.

Subject _____

    1. Book Title _____

        Call number _____   Page numbers _____

    2. Book Title _____

        Call number _____   Page numbers _____

Subject _____

    1. Book Title _____

        Call number _____   Page numbers _____

    2. Book Title _____

        Call number _____   Page numbers _____

Subject _____

    1. Book Title _____

        Call number _____   Page numbers _____

    2. Book Title _____

        Call number _____   Page numbers _____

Handout 4.2. Barbara K. Stripling and Judy M. Pitts, *Brainstorms and Blueprints: Teaching Library Research as a Thinking Process* (Englewood, Colo.: Libraries Unlimited, 1988).

BROWSING FOR TOPICS / *READERS' GUIDE*

Your name: _____

Period: _____

Dates covered by your *Readers' Guide*: _____

Directions: Look through the topics and subtopics in your *Readers' Guide*. Find two subjects which might interest someone in the class. Below, list the subjects and two articles with information about each subject. List only articles which should be available in this library.

Subject: _____

    1. Article Title: _____

        Magazine Title: _____

        Magazine Date: _____   Pages: _____

    2. Article Title: _____

        Magazine Title: _____

        Magazine Date: _____   Pages: _____

Subject: _____

    1. Article Title: _____

        Magazine Title: _____

        Magazine Date: _____   Pages: _____

    2. Article Title: _____

        Magazine Title: _____

        Magazine Date: _____   Pages: _____

Handout 4.3. Barbara K. Stripling and Judy M. Pitts, *Brainstorms and Blueprints: Teaching Library Research as a Thinking Process* (Englewood, Colo.: Libraries Unlimited, 1988).

Chapter 5

STEP TWO
Get an Overview of the Topic

"Susan, I didn't know you had study hall this period," Mr. Robinson, the library media specialist, paused beside the table, scanning the study hall pass for Susan's name.

Susan glanced up from the *Vogue* magazine she was studying. "I don't. My history teacher sent me to begin my research paper. I was absent yesterday when the class came in."

Mr. Robinson looked uncertainly at the *Vogue*. "Have you found what you need?"

"Nah. There isn't anything here on the topic Miss Elliot gave me. I'm going to ask her to give me another one." Susan turned back to the *Vogue*.

"What is your topic?"

"Some guys named Socko and Vincent. I looked them both up in the card catalog, but there's nothing." Susan flipped another magazine page.

"You're probably right. I don't think we have an entire book about Sacco and Vanzetti. You need to try a broader subject to find an overview. What kind of a book would have a chapter or a few paragraphs on them?"

Susan pondered Mr. Robinson's question, then brightened. "I know! I should have looked up RADIO."

"Radio?" Mr. Robinson was puzzled.

"Yes! Socko and Vincent were an early radio comedy team, weren't they?"

Too often, students share Susan's dilemma when they (and their teachers) forget the overview step of the research process. Research topics in teachers' general knowledge may confound students. Obviously, Susan will be frustrated if she searches books about radio for Socko and Vincent. If, on the other hand, she locates an overview of the Sacco and Vanzetti case, she will have enough basic knowledge to begin a research project successfully.

To complete this step of the research process, students must be able to:

1. Understand the concept of overview.

2. Begin a list of alternate subject headings to help locate an appropriate overview.

3. Locate the best overview for a particular subject/project.

4. Identify the central issues in an overview.

UNDERSTAND THE CONCEPT OF OVERVIEW

To introduce the idea of reading an overview before in-depth research, the teacher and library media specialist can offer a definition. An overview is a broad picture or summary of a subject; it contains information on who, what, where, when, why, and how. Students will go beyond learning a definition to recognizing the need for an overview when they begin trying to find information on their own topics.

BEGIN A LIST OF ALTERNATE SUBJECT HEADINGS

Because the overview will be the first information students attempt to locate, they should start compiling a list of alternate subject headings to guide their search. Generating these headings requires divergent thinking, expanding one's mind to new ideas. This skill determines the amount of information students can locate in the print collection or online databases.

Finding an overview and developing alternate subject headings often proceed concurrently. Susan would have difficulty determining alternate subject headings because she knows nothing about her assigned topic. In her case, locating the overview (with some professional assistance from Mr. Robinson) will have to come first. Other students, who understand their topic, can brainstorm alternate subject headings before searching for the overview. Without those headings, many students look up one subject only, find no information, and assume the library is woefully inadequate. Without subject headings skills, students will find *all* libraries woefully inadequate.

Teachers and library media specialists can require students to list a minimum of ten subject headings on a simple form during the course of their research (see handout 5.1). Usually the first reaction to this requirement is panic. A presentation by the teaching team on ways to *think of* subject headings can ease that panic. Later in the research process (see chapter 9), students can learn ways to *find* subject headings (by using cross references, for example).

Students write on the form their topic and the main word(s) of their subject. Then they use three ways to *think of* additional subject headings—thinking of broader terms, narrower terms, and related terms or synonyms.

Choosing the Main Word

While it seems simple to identify main words, topics expressed in a phrase or statement often pose problems for students. Given the topic "causes of stress," a surprising number of students will choose "causes" as the first word they should look up. Names also prove difficult for some students who will search for a first instead of last name.

Topics with more than one main word also cause problems. A subject such as "uses of helicopters in the Vietnam conflict" will require students to locate information about helicopters that includes facts about Vietnam, and vice versa. The topic "dogs in police work" may be found under both "dogs" and "police." A Venn diagram will help illustrate this concept of dual main words.

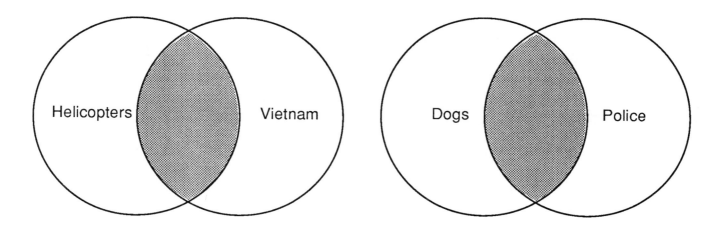

(See handout 5.2 for a transparency master to provide practice in choosing main word(s).)

Moving to a Broader Term

To perform this step, students must categorize their topic. Given a few examples, most students understand broader terms. A bull's-eye can help students visualize this concept.

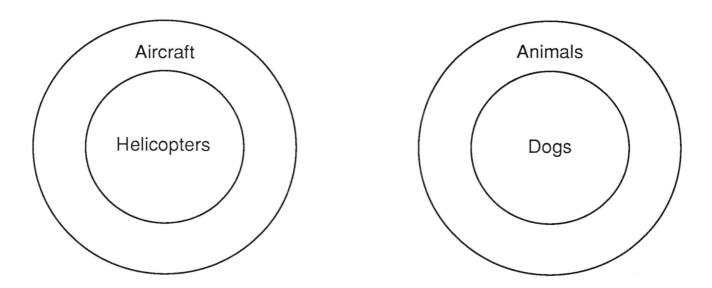

Broader terms will be especially useful for the card catalog. Library media specialists can lead students to broader terms by asking, "If we don't have a whole book on helicopters, a book on what subject would most likely contain information on helicopters?"

Moving to a Narrower Term

To think of narrower terms, students must break a subject into smaller parts. Working through several narrowing diagrams will usually give students adequate guidance in this process.

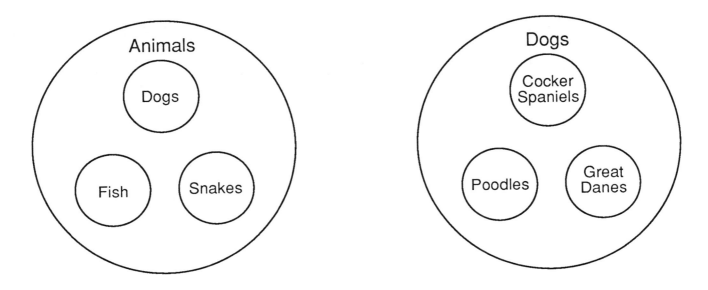

Narrower terms will be especially useful for magazine indexes like the *Readers' Guide* and book indexes.

Listing a Synonym or Related Term

Most secondary students understand the concept of "synonym." Those who do not may be helped with a diagram.

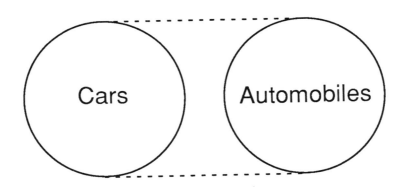

Students are surprised that many subjects do not have synonyms.

Related terms are more complicated than synonyms. They represent ideas that are associated with the subject but are not exact synonyms. For the topic "anorexia nervosa," additional information can be found under the related term "bulimia."

Teaching the Subject Heading Process

Students can practice thinking of subject headings with a small-group activity that uses outdated telephone directory Yellow Pages. (These are often available from local telephone companies or can be scavenged from schools and homes when new books appear.) Discussion following the exercise should center on the subject heading strategies used to locate the answer to each question (see handout 5.3).

Using a transparency of the subject headings worksheet (handout 5.1), teachers can model the process of beginning a list of alternate subject headings. Examples might include:

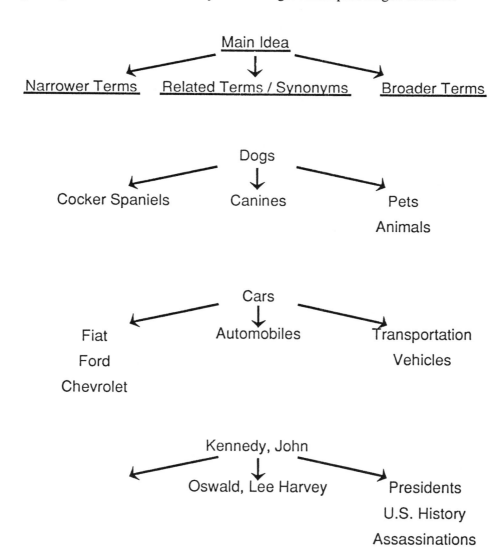

Students need not think of subject headings for all three columns immediately. Additional terms can be added as the research progresses. All the techniques may not work for each topic. For example, there is no synonym for "Kennedy, John."

Once teachers have modeled the process, they can ask students to offer their own topics for class development of subject headings. After working through a few examples, students can begin their own list. Armed with their headings, students are ready to locate an overview.

LOCATE THE BEST OVERVIEW FOR A PARTICULAR SUBJECT/PROJECT

Students can obtain an overview in more than one way. Sometimes the classroom teacher and textbook provide it before students begin research in the library media center. If students must locate their overview, they may use general and subject encyclopedias, other reference books, and magazines. Occasionally, students must read more widely than a single source to acquire overview information.

Using Reference Materials for the Overview

If students have little basic knowledge about their topic and if the assigned project is short, a general encyclopedia is the best source for background information. Ironically, some teachers, hoping to raise their students' research level beyond the copying-from-the-encyclopedia stage, forbid use of a general encyclopedia. Those students may spend several days discovering information (such as their topic's chronological and geographical limits or even the correct spelling of names) readily available in a general encyclopedia.

Although a general encyclopedia is an excellent source of overviews for many topics, students may not be able to locate the information easily. In the index they should try several subject headings from their list to locate all the pertinent information. Students who are researching teenage suicide may not find an article specifically on that topic. The broader subject heading of "suicide" will yield an article which may provide necessary overview facts such as the following:

Who: Those at risk for suicide.

What: Definition of suicide; statistics.

When: Changes in teen suicide rates over the last twenty-five years.

Why: Personal and social reasons for suicide.

Students will find that general encyclopedias differ in their coverage of topics. A quick review of three articles on suicide reveals the following differences in length alone: *Academic American Encyclopedia* (1986), twelve paragraphs; *Encyclopedia Americana* (1982), ten paragraphs; *World Book Encyclopedia* (1983), four paragraphs.

The information within the articles will also vary. The most specific information on teenage suicide can be found in the *Academic American* article. Students should check more than one encyclopedia before taking overview notes. They can analyze the articles by answering the following questions:

1. How long is the article?

2. Is the whole article or only a part of it on your subject?

3. Does the article include historical background as well as the current situation?

4. Does the article contain helpful definitions, identifications, and statistics?

5. How current is the encyclopedia? Is your topic one that requires the most current information?

6. Does the article answer several of the following: who, what, where, when, why, and how?

If the class needs further discussion on the differences among encyclopedias, teachers can hand out copies of different articles on the same topic, prepare transparencies of the articles, or assign reading of the articles in the library media center prior to discussion.

Some students will need more than one encyclopedia to locate adequate overview information; others will discover that an overview may not be available in a general encyclopedia. "Teenage pregnancy" yields little information even under the related term "adolescence" and the broader term "pregnancy." Excellent information is available in other reference sources on adolescence or health and medicine. The library media specialist may assist students in locating these sources.

Using Magazines for the Overview

Some students choose topics too current for even the latest set of general encyclopedias. When anorexia nervosa and AIDS first received wide coverage in national media, many students wanted to research those subjects. Neither topic was covered in a general encyclopedia or any books found in typical school library media centers. One to two years elapsed before encyclopedia articles or books were readily available.

Despite the dearth of books with information on anorexia nervosa or AIDS, both topics were acceptable for research because they were adequately covered in magazines. In cases like these, students will have to locate overview information in magazines.

Locating a magazine article containing overview information requires some special skills. Once students have discovered the correct subject heading to use in the magazine index or electronic database, they face several article citations. Many students simply start at the beginning of the list, trying to locate articles.

Instead, students should browse the entries, using critical thinking to predict which articles will provide an overview. Before deciding, they can consider three items in each entry: the article title, the magazine title, and the article length.

The article title is the best indicator of the content. *Readers' Guide*, for the past few years, has been adding additional information (in brackets) if the title is unclear. By browsing through all the titles, students can guess which articles contain background information. Students working on the topic "surrogate mothers" may find the following article titles:

"I Had to Pay Another Woman to Have My Baby"

"The Battle over Baby M"

"Surrogate Motherhood [Special Section]"

"A Split Decision [custody suit filed by surrogate mother]"

Of the four articles listed, three obviously deal with specific cases and may even be first-person accounts. Only the third article is about surrogate motherhood in general; by locating and skimming the actual article, students can ascertain whether it provides an overview.

While considering the article titles, students should also think about the magazine titles. As a rule, the more specialized the magazine, the less likely it is to include overview information because typical readers already possess necessary background knowledge. Students searching for overview information about compact disc players may find articles listed in *High Fidelity, Stereo Review*, and *New Republic*. The first two magazines offer articles about specific new developments or products; the third, a more general news magazine, is likely to provide an overview.

Students who locate more than one overview article can then consider the length of the article as a criterion. Experienced researchers save time by choosing the longer articles first.

If many students in a particular class are researching current topics, teachers and library media specialists should present the above information to the entire class. If only a few students have chosen current topics, they can be helped individually.

Reading Widely for the Overview

Students working on research at a level higher than simple fact-finding or questioning / searching may need a more in-depth overview than a single encyclopedia or magazine article. They may use several sources for background information.

These students gather a variety of materials (books, reference sources, magazine articles) related to their subject. They use tables of contents or article subheads to locate appropriate sections to peruse. They do not read every word, nor do they take notes other than those necessary to remember a concept, name, spelling, date, or location for later research.

After skimming through a source, students jot down ideas generated by their reading—their understandings and their questions. The students are not reproducing the information from the source; rather they are building background knowledge and generating their own concepts to provide a framework for narrowing the topic in the next step of the research process.

Starting a Working Bibliography

Once satisfactory overview information has been located, students set up their working bibliography. Because many students feel uncomfortable with bibliographic style, the library media specialist can work through a sample bibliographic entry with the class. The students use the sample as a guide, inserting the correct information from their own overview source(s).

IDENTIFY THE CENTRAL ISSUES IN AN OVERVIEW

Once they have located an overview, students must decide what they need to learn from it. A simple notetaking sheet can guide those using a reference source or a magazine article (see handout 5.4).

For low-level research, the central issues are the "who," "what," "where," "when," "why," and "how" facts. The "who" includes individuals, groups, and organizations that seem prominent. The overview article on suicide described those at risk. The "what" information includes definitions, major points, and statistics. For suicide, that included a definition and statistics. In a similar manner, the "where," "when," "why," and "how" information will be in the overview if they are important to the subject.

Students performing high-level research, who have read widely for their overview, may find that their central issues go beyond the "who-and-what" information. They can identify those issues by brainstorming.

As a model, teachers can show students a sample brainstormed list of central issues for a high-level topic. An American history teacher may select the topic "the 1960s: decade of ferment." For this subject, the central issues include:

Blacks split between nonviolence and militance.

Youths resist the draft.

Political assassinations affect society.

Women demand rights.

Hippies drop out.

Vietnam war displayed on television.

Drug use increases.

Youths protest on college campuses.

More American troops sent to Vietnam.

The students may practice brainstorming central issues on topics already surveyed in class. After brainstorming, the class works through the resulting list to ensure that every item is an appropriate and thoughtful central issue.

COMPENSATION FOR THIS STEP

Obtaining an overview is essential to the research process. The overview provides basic information the students will need to continue the research and gives them a focus for narrowing the topic in the next step of the process.

While the step cannot be skipped, teachers can provide the overview by lecturing on the broad subject or by assigning textbook readings. These activities should take place before students begin narrowing their research topic.

Name: _____   Period: _____

SUBJECT HEADINGS WORKSHEET

During your research, write the subject headings you have used.
List at least *ten* subject headings.

TOPIC: _____

_____
[main word(s) to look up]

Narrower Terms   Related Terms / Synonyms   Broader Terms

Handout 5.1. Barbara K. Stripling and Judy M. Pitts, *Brainstorms and Blueprints: Teaching Library Research as a Thinking Process* (Englewood, Colo.: Libraries Unlimited, 1988).

CHOOSING THE MAIN WORD

Circle the main word (the first word you should look up) in the topics below.

1. History of Jazz

2. Training Techniques for Horses

3. Architecture in Colonial America

4. Women's Rights

5. Choosing the Best Diet

The topics below may have more than one main word. Circle one *or* two words to begin looking up for each topic.

6. Chemical Warfare in the Modern World

7. Marijuana and Cocaine: America's Twin Dilemmas

8. The Influence of Elvis Presley on Today's Music

9. Helping Children Confront Death

10. The Threat of Nuclear Winter

Suggested answers are on page 52.

Handout 5.2. Barbara K. Stripling and Judy M. Pitts, *Brainstorms and Blueprints: Teaching Library Research as a Thinking Process* (Englewood, Colo.: Libraries Unlimited, 1988).

NAME THAT SUBJECT HEADING

Each problem below could be solved with a telephone call. Your task is to figure out *what subject headings in the Yellow Pages* will lead to the correct phone numbers.

For each problem:

1) Circle the main word(s) to look up first.
2) List the other subject headings you try. Your last subject heading should be the one that works.
3) Label each subject heading as BT (Broader Term), NT (Narrower Term), or RT (Related Term/Synonym).

Example: You are getting married in six months. You need to order announcements.

Main Word: (Announcements)

Other Subject Headings	*Type*
Invitations	RT
Marriage	BT
Wedding Announcements	NT

1. You have just inherited $1,000,000. You need to see a lawyer about setting up a trust fund.

2. Your home tap water has a peculiar taste. You want to call the Water Department to find out what's wrong.

3. You think you must have an allergy because you're sneezing and wheezing. You want to call an allergy doctor.

4. You need to call the high school to tell the principal you can't make it to detention.

5. You want to know when all the movies in town start.

6. You need to reach your mother at the roller rink.

7. You want to find a job so you can buy a car. You haven't had any luck on your own, so you decide to enlist professional help.

8. Your car died at the corner down the street. You need to call a car repair service.

9. You want to write to your Aunt Tisha but you've lost her zip code. You need to call the post office.

10. You want to redo your room. Your mother says that you can hire a decorator to help.

Suggested answers are on page 52.

Handout 5.3. Barbara K. Stripling and Judy M. Pitts, *Brainstorms and Blueprints: Teaching Library Research as a Thinking Process* (Englewood, Colo.: Libraries Unlimited, 1988).

Suggested answers for handout 5.2.

1. Jazz

2. Horses

3. Architecture

4. Women

5. Diet

6. Chemical; Warfare

7. Marijuana; Cocaine

8. Presley; Music

9. Children; Death

10. Nuclear

Sample answers (telephone subject headings may vary) to handout 5.3.

1. Lawyer = main word; Attorneys = RT

2. Water Department = main words; Government - City = BT

3. Doctor = main word; Physicians & Surgeons - M.D. = RT

4. High School = main words; Schools - Public = BT

5. Movies = main word; Theatres = RT

6. Roller Rink = main words; Skating Rinks = RT

7. Job = main word; Employment Agencies = RT

8. Car Repair = main words; Automobile Repairing & Service = RT

9. Post Office = main words; Government - United States = BT

10. Decorator = main word; Interior Decorators & Designers = RT

NAME _____ PERIOD _____

OVERVIEW NOTE SHEET

TOPIC: _____

SOURCE: _____
(Example: *World Book*, Vol. 6, p. 9)

Take notes on the *Who, What, Where, When, Why,* and *How* ideas that are important to your topic.

Page	Notes

Handout 5.4. Barbara K. Stripling and Judy M. Pitts, *Brainstorms and Blueprints: Teaching Library Research as a Thinking Process* (Englewood, Colo.: Libraries Unlimited, 1988).

Chapter 6

STEP THREE
Narrow the Topic

Matt could "blend into the woodwork." He never caused trouble, usually turned in his assignments, performed adequately, and learned enough to get by.

On this November Thursday, Matt was uneasy. His class was researching, and for some reason, the library media specialist, Miss Turner, kept noticing him. He had deflected her inquiries two days earlier by choosing a broad topic—World War II. Then yesterday he'd found an overview. He'd get the encyclopedia again today; that should keep her off his back.

As innocuously as possible, Matt hunched over the open encyclopedia in his well-practiced, ready-to-work-but-not-so-excited-I-want-to-talk-about-it position.

"Uh, oh," Matt sighed. "Here she comes again."

"Hi, Matt. How's the research coming?" Miss Turner pulled up a chair.

"Oh, fine."

"Have you decided how you want to narrow your topic, Matt?"

"Yeah, I'm all set. I'm going to do World War II," Matt replied politely.

"World War II is too broad for a three-page paper. We need to narrow. Have you found anything that particularly interests you about World War II?" Miss Turner's eyes pressed for an answer.

"No, I want to do World War II."

"But, Matt, whole books have been written about World War II. You can't possibly cover that much information. Let me help you find a narrower topic about World War II."

"I *know* there are books about World War II; I've found them. That's why I want to do my paper on that topic." Matt was frustrated at Miss Turner's persistence. What did she want him to do? Pick a topic he'd have to look for?

Matt's resistance to narrowing follows the pattern of many student researchers. They realize that the more they narrow, the less information they will find and assume that narrowing will make the research difficult.

In reality, narrow topics are easier to research than broad. First, by focusing their topic, students set boundaries on the information they need which will help them locate it efficiently. Second, they will not be overwhelmed by the amount of information available and can concentrate on particular chapters or pages rather than whole books. With less material to peruse, students will be able to evaluate the information.

Third, students with narrow topics will be likely to discover specific details to enliven a researched subject because they are freed from having to summarize huge amounts of information. A project limited to "epidemics in pre-Revolutionary America" can reveal that a smallpox epidemic in 1721 in Boston infected over fifty percent of the population and killed one out of seven people; that smallpox inoculation was first successfully practiced by Dr. Zabdiel Boylston in 1721; and that smallpox inoculations were opposed by a physician, William Douglass, who then died of smallpox in 1752 (facts chosen from Morris, Richard B., ed., *Encyclopedia of American History* [New York: Harper & Row, 1976]).

Such specific details can be featured in a project limited to epidemics in pre-Revolutionary America. With the broader topic of "everyday life in pre-Revolutionary America," students have so much information to cover that most of their paper is not lively details, but generalizations: "One of the problems for the colonists was widespread disease."

Unfortunately, some students can become overzealous and narrow too much. The library media specialist or teacher can reject unresearchable gems like "the early development of paper clips" or "the nutritional properties of ice cream."

Students need practice both in recognizing acceptably narrowed topics and in narrowing a variety of topics so that they will feel competent to limit any subject. They must be able to:

1. Distinguish broad from narrow topics.

2. Develop narrow topics from a broad topic.

3. Relate topic choice to assigned length of project.

4. Understand various ways of narrowing—to a problem or question; topically; chronologically; geographically.

DISTINGUISH BROAD FROM NARROW TOPICS

Many secondary students have difficulty distinguishing broad from narrow ideas. Practice in arranging topics in broad to narrow order helps them recognize that related topics have varying degrees of narrowness (see handout 6.1).

DEVELOP NARROW TOPICS FROM A BROAD TOPIC

In addition to distinguishing broad from narrow topics, students must also be able to generate narrow topics for a chosen research area. Overview information will provide the departure point for this narrowing. Students who used a reference source or magazine will have identified their subject's main ideas. Others, who read widely and detected issues beyond the "who-where-what," will need to categorize their ideas before narrowing. The following central issues for the broad research area of the 1960s (presented as a sample in chapter 5) now have categories added.

List of Issues	*Category*
Blacks split between nonviolence and militance.	Civil Rights
Youths resist the draft.	Youth Unrest
Political assassinations affect society.	Assassinations
Women demand rights.	Civil Rights
Hippies drop out.	Alternative Lifestyles
Vietnam war displayed on television.	Vietnam War
Drug use increases.	Alternative Lifestyles
Youths protest on college campuses.	Youth Unrest
More American troops sent to Vietnam.	Vietnam War

With their central issues in mind, students can use a clustering activity to narrow their topic. Students place their broad topic in the center of the page with their main ideas around it.

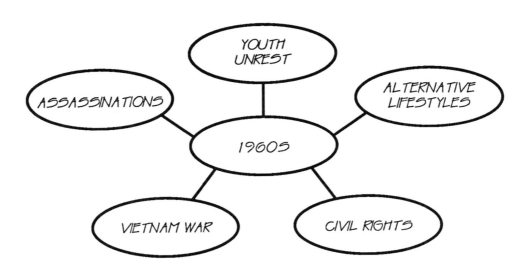

Next, they select one of the radiated ideas to be the nucleus of a new cluster.

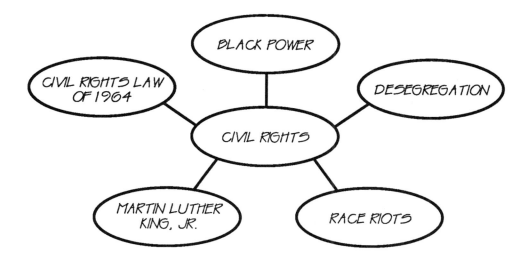

Students then choose one or two areas to pursue with continued clustering and narrow progressively until they identify several viable research topics.

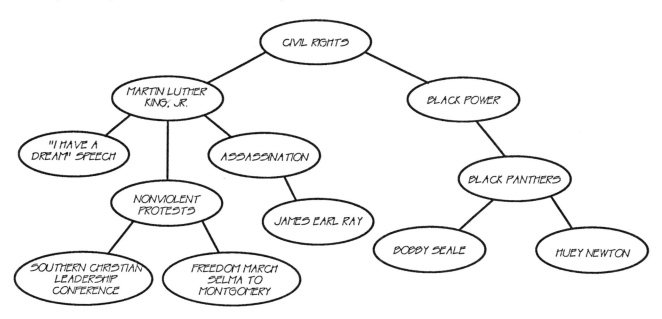

RELATE TOPIC CHOICE TO ASSIGNED LENGTH OF PROJECT

Students have trouble relating their topic choice to the length of their project. Instead of narrowing their topic to fit the assigned project length, many students stay with a broad topic and scribble enough superficial information to fill the required pages. They choose a topic like "medical research" for a three-page paper and write three pages worth of general information. Instead, the goal should be to choose a topic which will allow in-depth communication of all aspects within the length allowed. As the students narrow, they should ask: Can I convey a sound understanding and specific details about my topic in the space that I have?

Students can develop an ability to relate topic choice to project length by examining lists of topics and determining how long a project would be necessary to cover each of the topics (see handout 6.2). Teachers should follow the individual activity with class discussion since students may be able to justify different answers.

UNDERSTAND VARIOUS WAYS OF NARROWING

Some students may discover that, even though they have narrowed their topic with clusters, they still do not have a narrow enough topic. These students can try four techniques for narrowing: narrowing to a problem or question; narrowing topically; narrowing chronologically; narrowing geographically.

Narrowing to a Problem or Question

Students who restrict their topic to a problem or question are led to perform thoughtful research. These students can use the lists of verbs at different reaction levels in chapter 2 to help them construct their question or problem. If Sally's chosen broad topic is fashion, she might narrow to a question on any of the six thought levels:

Level 1 (fact-finding): What characteristics would *identify* women's fashions in the 1920s?

Level 2 (asking / searching): How could the major trends in nineteenth-century children's fashions be *described* and *illustrated*?

Level 3 (examining / organizing): How were fashions in the 1960s *related* to the mood of the country?

Level 4 (evaluating / deliberating): How can the fashion industry *defend* the practice of changing the styles and colors every year?

Level 5 (integrating / concluding): Based on American society and the fashion industry today, what fashion trends can be *predicted* for the next ten years?

Level 6 (conceptualizing): What new women's fashion line could I *design* which would incorporate my knowledge of fashion cycles, my predictions for the country's immediate economic and social future, and my understanding of marketing strategies?

Narrowing Topically

Most subtopics that students have brainstormed and clustered are examples of topical narrowing. In the above fashion examples, topical narrowing led to *children's* fashions, *styles* and *colors* of fashion changes, and investigating the *mood* rather than the politics or economics of the country.

Narrowing Chronologically

Almost any topic beyond a simple definition can be narrowed by time. The time boundaries will vary according to the subject, length of the project, and distance from present day. "Fashion during the Renaissance" would cover at least a one-hundred-year time span. Because more information would be available, recent fashion would be limited to a decade or perhaps a single year.

Narrowing Geographically

Many topics can be narrowed to a country, a state or region, a city, or any other specific location (rain forests, New York City subways). Most students naturally (and unthinkingly) limit their topics to the United States because most sources in American school libraries also have that bias. Teachers and library media specialists should help students choose geographical limitations or be aware of the limitations implied by their topic.

Using Combinations of Narrowing Techniques

Students may use a combination of techniques to narrow their topics. All of the fashion topic questions listed above employ at least two ways to narrow. By combining techniques, students can limit their topics to those that can be effective within the limits of the assignment. Giving students practice in narrowing can help them learn to combine techniques (see handout 6.3).

COMPENSATION FOR THIS STEP

Narrowing the topic may be skipped by the students if the teacher or library media specialist assigns narrow topics or provides a choice of narrow topics. Teachers who want to ensure that every aspect of a curricular unit is researched should consider assigning the narrow topics.

If the students have relative freedom of topic choice, but the teacher or library media specialist does not have time for narrowing activities, the students can use topic selection books. Two that have proven helpful for secondary students are the Lamm and Powell books included in the bibliography.

REFLECTION POINT
Is my topic a good one?

After students have narrowed their topic, they should evaluate their choice before continuing the research. The student should ask:

1. Am I really interested in the subject?

2. Can I convey a sound understanding and specific details in the space I have?

3. Is it probable that there will be enough information available?

4. Will the information be too difficult to use?

5. Final check: Is the subject too broad? too narrow? too subjective? too unfamiliar? too difficult?

If students are unable to answer the reflection-point questions satisfactorily, they should work through the previous research steps again until they are confident their narrow topic will lead to successful research. Students who look backward to evaluate their progress are capable of looking forward to control their research directions. This self-guidance is a high-level skill which leads to flexibility and a willingness to change, attitudes essential for successful researchers.

BROAD TO NARROW TOPICS

Directions: Number each group of topics in broad to narrow order. (1 = broad)

_____	Civil rights cases	_____	FAA regulations
_____	*Brown v. Board of Education*	_____	Aviation
_____	Desegregation	_____	Air traffic controllers
_____	Titanic	_____	Basketball
_____	Disasters	_____	Final Four
_____	Shipwrecks	_____	NCAA
_____	Wild West	_____	Bubonic plague
_____	Jesse James	_____	Medical history
_____	Gunfighters	_____	Epidemics
_____	Mass murderers	_____	Acid rain
_____	Crime	_____	Pollution
_____	Charles Manson	_____	Ecology
_____	Euthanasia	_____	Chemical warfare
_____	Karen Ann Quinlan	_____	Agent Orange
_____	Death	_____	Defoliants

Suggested answers are on page 63.

Handout 6.1. Barbara K. Stripling and Judy M. Pitts, *Brainstorms and Blueprints: Teaching Library Research as a Thinking Process* (Englewood, Colo.: Libraries Unlimited, 1988).

RELATING TOPIC CHOICE TO LENGTH OF PROJECT

Which of the following could best be covered in a paragraph (P), three-page essay (E), 15-page research paper (RP), or book (B)?

1. _____ Definition of hologram
2. _____ Causes of liver cirrhosis
3. _____ Marriage customs in China
4. _____ Toxic waste
5. _____ Invention of the ballpoint pen
6. _____ Sinking of the Lusitania
7. _____ Handwriting analysis
8. _____ Nightmares
9. _____ Claustrophobia
10. _____ Medieval architecture
11. _____ Mercy killing
12. _____ Origin of Valentine's Day
13. _____ Lindbergh kidnapping law
14. _____ 3-D movies
15. _____ Pony Express
16. _____ Definition of idiot savant
17. _____ Warning signs for teenage suicide
18. _____ Photography
19. _____ Language of facial expressions
20. _____ Great Depression

Suggested answers are on page 63.

Handout 6.2. Barbara K. Stripling and Judy M. Pitts, *Brainstorms and Blueprints: Teaching Library Research as a Thinking Process* (Englewood, Colo.: Libraries Unlimited, 1988).

Suggested answers for handout 6.1.

BROAD TO NARROW TOPICS

Directions: Number each group of topics in broad to narrow order. (1 = broad)

__2__	Civil rights cases		__2__	FAA regulations
__3__	*Brown v. Board of Education*		__1__	Aviation
__1__	Desegregation		__3__	Air traffic controllers
__3__	Titanic		__2__	Basketball
__1__	Disasters		__3__	Final Four
__2__	Shipwrecks		__1__	NCAA
__1__	Wild West		__3__	Bubonic plague
__3__	Jesse James		__1__	Medical history
__2__	Gunfighters		__2__	Epidemics
__2__	Mass murderers		__3__	Acid rain
__1__	Crime		__2__	Pollution
__3__	Charles Manson		__1__	Ecology
__2__	Euthanasia		__1__	Chemical warfare
__3__	Karen Ann Quinlan		__3__	Agent Orange
__1__	Death		__2__	Defoliants

Suggested answers for handout 6.2, "Relating Topic Choice to Length of Project."

Although the length of each of the above research projects is open to discussion, the following answers would certainly be acceptable: (1) P; (2) E; (3) RP; (4) B; (5) P; (6) RP; (7) RP; (8) RP; (9) E; (10) B; (11) RP; (12) P; (13) E; (14) RP; (15) RP; (16) P; (17) E; (18) B; (19) RP; (20) B.

NARROWING A TOPIC

Narrow each broad topic below using the four techniques for narrowing: topically, chronologically, geographically, by a problem or question. Use a combination where necessary.

Example: Motion Pictures
    Topically: <u>Walt Disney feature length cartoons</u>
    Chronologically: <u>The big studio system of the 1930s</u>
    Geographically: <u>The Cannes Film Festival</u>
    Problem or question: <u>How do film comedies of today compare to early silent film comedies?</u>

Basketball
    Topically: _____
    Chronologically: _____
    Geographically: _____
    Problem or question: _____

Aviation
    Topically: _____
    Chronologically: _____
    Geographically: _____
    Problem or question: _____

Fashion
    Topically: _____
    Chronologically: _____
    Geographically: _____
    Problem or question: _____

Television
    Topically: _____
    Chronologically: _____
    Geographically: _____
    Problem or question: _____

Divorce
    Topically: _____
    Chronologically: _____
    Geographically: _____
    Problem or question: _____

Diets

    Topically: _____

    Chronologically: _____

    Geographically: _____

    Problem or question: _____

Sleep

    Topically: _____

    Chronologically: _____

    Geographically: _____

    Problem or question: _____

Brain

    Topically: _____

    Chronologically: _____

    Geographically: _____

    Problem or question: _____

Child Abuse

    Topically: _____

    Chronologically: _____

    Geographically: _____

    Problem or question: _____

Terrorism

    Topically: _____

    Chronologically: _____

    Geographically: _____

    Problem or question: _____

Crime

    Topically: _____

    Chronologically: _____

    Geographically: _____

    Problem or question: _____

Mental illness

    Topically: _____

    Chronologically: _____

    Geographically: _____

    Problem or question: _____

Handout 6.3. Barbara K. Stripling and Judy M. Pitts, *Brainstorms and Blueprints: Teaching Library Research as a Thinking Process* (Englewood, Colo.: Libraries Unlimited, 1988).

Chapter 7

STEP FOUR AND STEP FIVE
Develop a Thesis and
Formulate Questions

As soon as the bell rang, Steven dug in his pocket for his perennial pencil stub, flipped open the encyclopedia he had already retrieved from the reference section, and announced, "OK. I'm ready to research now."

"Good, Steven. I'm glad you're so eager to start." The library media specialist sat beside him and spoke quietly while the teacher began taking roll. "Let me see the thesis you wrote last night."

"I don't need to do that thesis thing you talked about yesterday. I already know what I'm going to research—boxing in the United States. See all this stuff I found?" Steven proudly displayed his "boxing" encyclopedia article.

"But what do you plan to learn about boxing?"

"You know, just boxing." Steven's voice was tinged with impatience. "There's plenty of stuff here."

Steven *has* found "plenty of stuff" (at least in one source), but he is setting himself up to fail. He has identified only a broad topic and will probably produce a shallow "report." He wants to complete the assignment easily rather than to learn and communicate new information about a specific aspect of his topic.

Steps four and five of the research process (developing a thesis statement and writing questions), combined with careful determination of the research level by the teachers, propel students beyond Steven's simple fact-finding. Students should perform these two steps together, perhaps within the same activity. The questions evolve from the thesis, and the two together provide a foundation and framework to support thoughtful research.

While students at any intellectual and developmental level can complete these steps, those in low-level classes or in early junior high will need direct guidance, perhaps including specific wording suggestions. Students in more advanced classes will need encouragement. Often this is the first time they have been asked to develop a framework for their own learning, and many fear they cannot do so.

Step Four: Develop a Thesis or Statement of Purpose

To complete this step of the research process, students must be able to:

1. Understand the concept of *thesis* or *statement of purpose.*

2. Clarify the major focus of their own research in a one-sentence thesis or statement of purpose.

UNDERSTAND CONCEPT OF THESIS OR STATEMENT OF PURPOSE

Defining Thesis or Statement of Purpose

A *thesis* is an overall goal, a controlling idea. For a research project, a thesis is a declarative statement of the main idea which can be supported by evidence. An example is "Stress, a condition which can seriously threaten an individual's health in a variety of ways, can be alleviated with personal health care techniques." The thesis can be compared to a topic sentence in a paragraph, a structure most students understand. In fact, the thesis statement often serves as the topic sentence for both the introductory paragraph and the entire project.

A *statement of purpose* is more personal and informal than a thesis. It simply presents the researcher's intent, often using the word "I." "I plan to research the causes of stress and its effects on the body. I will also present stress-reduction techniques." The statement of purpose guides the research, but it is too informal and researcher-centered to be included in the final product.

Recognizing Theses in Essays and Projects

To be able to write a clearly stated controlling idea, students must be able to distinguish a thesis statement someone else has created from a simple fact (see handout 7.1). The concept of thesis statement can be emphasized at any time in the classroom when students read a supplemental article or view an audiovisual resource. They can analyze the product and find or compose a brief statement of the main idea. This analysis, practiced over a period of time, will teach students the skill of focusing on the producer's main point (important for the subject matter being studied) by recognizing the thesis statement.

CLARIFY THE MAJOR FOCUS OF THE RESEARCH IN A THESIS OR STATEMENT OF PURPOSE

Professional writers/producers always start a project by clarifying their focus. Beginning writers/producers must do the same. By this step of the research process, most students can identify their opinions and their specific areas of interest about their subject; they must now shape these into a structure to provide an organization and a focused main idea. Once students commit their goals to paper as a thesis or statement of purpose, teachers can detect vague or grandiose thinking and insist that students sharpen their focus.

Statement of Purpose

Because the statement of purpose is informal and easier to write than a thesis, it is more appropriate for younger students or for those performing simple research. To give students practice throughout the year in writing statements of purpose (and also to help them develop a stock of topics for upcoming research assignments), teachers can ask class members to write individual statements of purpose about topics that they are studying.

If a child development class has been discussing learning problems, students might develop statements such as "I would like to research the relationship between hearing problems and speech development" or "I am interested in children's reading problems, especially in dyslexia." A list of statements of purpose maintained over several weeks of class will provide students with a choice of topics and controlling statements when they begin a research project.

The statement of purpose can be helpful even if a thesis is required; many students find that first writing a statement of purpose clarifies their thoughts. In fact, they can brainstorm three or four statements of purpose which can be combined and adapted into the formal thesis.

Thesis Statement

Students can learn to write a thesis statement in a controlled classroom situation. The teacher gives all students the same set of facts and asks each student to write a thesis (see handout 7.2). Discussing and revising the resulting thesis statements will help students see the number of successful theses that can be written for the same subject. Students will also benefit from participating in whole-class development of thesis statements for a few research topics chosen by the students.

Teachers may discover that some students' first theses are unusable. These usually fall into one of three problem types. First, the problem thesis may be a simple statement of fact, such as a definition, which needs no support. Steven, featured at the beginning of this chapter, would produce that type of thesis if he wrote, "Boxing is a contact sport" (see handout 7.1).

Second, some theses are personal opinions based on emotion rather than reason: "Boxing is a useless, violent sport." Students with emotional theses will find critical research difficult because they will be looking only for information to support their emotional stand.

Finally, a problem thesis may be a self-evident statement of truth such as "Boxing can be dangerous." Some of these can be made successful by adding more information: "Boxing's popularity depends on the danger involved and the expectation of injury."

Thesis Statements and Research Levels

When writing a thesis statement, students should incorporate the critical thinking that has been specified by their assignment. To help students reach the right level of thought, teachers can offer some guiding nouns (converted from the verbs listed for the research levels in chapter 2). If students are working toward the third level (examining / organizing), their thesis should indicate that they will produce an analysis, classification, interpretation, modification, organization, solution, verification, etc.

Below are thesis statements about stress for the different levels of research.

Fact-finding

Stress is both a psychological and a physical problem. (Definition)

Asking / Searching

Stress among adolescents can be attributed to factors in the home, the environment of the school, and the personality of the individual. (Explanation)

Examining / Organizing

The rate of stress-related diseases among women in the United States is steadily increasing because of the increase in the employment level among women. (Examination)

Evaluating / Deliberating

Most treatments for stress are ineffective because stress is treated as a physical or mental problem instead of an environmental or social problem. (Evaluation)

Integrating / Concluding

Stress-related diseases will continue to increase until the "yuppie, drive-for-success" syndrome cycles out. (Prediction)

Conceptualizing

Corporations should set up a model program for employee stress reduction that involves flexible scheduling, physical fitness, day-care provision, and employee decision making. (Development of a model program)

No matter how the thesis is developed, its wording should remain flexible. Students may change the emphasis after they locate research materials; many will refine the wording for final inclusion in the project.

REFLECTION POINT
Does my thesis or statement of purpose represent an effective, overall concept for my research?

Students should consider the following:

1. Statement of purpose: Does my statement of purpose provide a clear focus for my research?
   Thesis: Is my thesis a declarative statement of the main idea which can be supported by evidence? Or is it: a simple statement of fact needing no support? a personal opinion based on emotion rather than reason? a self-evident statement of truth?

2. Will my thesis or statement of purpose lead to the level of research that fits the assignment?

Step Five: Formulate Questions to Guide Research

To complete this step of the research process, students must be able to:

1. Write questions that fulfill the thesis or statement of purpose.

2. Write questions that lead to the appropriate level of research.

3. Continue using questions throughout the research.

WRITE QUESTIONS THAT FULFILL THESIS OR
STATEMENT OF PURPOSE

Once students have laid a foundation for their research with their thesis or statement of purpose, they are ready to construct the framework by writing research questions. Because the questions provide the structure necessary to prove the controlling idea, they must be written *after* the thesis or statement of purpose. Students often try to reverse the steps.

Questioning is an important critical thinking skill which can deepen understanding of any information; yet, students are often uncomfortable asking questions. Their usual role in the educational process is *answering* questions, not posing them (Schaffer, 1987).

As students write questions to guide their research, they should consider several factors. First, the questions should interest them so that they will not merely grab-bag answers to satisfy the teacher. Second, the questions should take into account the information needed by the audience/reader to understand the topic. Finally, every question must lead to answers that will support the thesis or statement of purpose.

The number of questions that should be written depends on the complexity of the research project. Most simple to moderate projects require no more than six to nine questions, and in fact, students sometimes have trouble juggling more than that. Students ready for high levels of research can work with more questions.

WRITE QUESTIONS THAT LEAD TO THE APPROPRIATE
LEVEL OF RESEARCH

Question Categories for Factual Information

To help students develop questions for simple research projects (levels 1, 2, 3), teachers can provide categories for questions ranging from factual to more complex.

1. *Overview Information/Statistics/Definitions*
    Basic information audience/reader will need
    Who? What? Where? When?

2. *Background/Causes/Reasons*
    Details needed to understand issues fully
    How? Why?

3. *Effects/Solutions/Recommended Changes*
    Projections made from or found within the information
    What if?

Interpretive Questions Leading to Conclusions

At the high levels of research, students begin with the same factual questions, then expand to those that direct their research toward the type of conclusions they expect to reach.

Hypothesis—What would happen if some circumstance about the subject had been different or were changed?

Prediction—Based on the evidence collected, what will happen in the future?

Solution—What possible solution(s) could be offered to solve the problems identified by the research?

Comparison or analogy—In what ways does the researched subject compare to similar subjects or to the same subject in a different era?

Judgment—What final evaluation (supported by research) can be made about the subject?

Answers to these high-level, interpretive, and evaluative questions will not usually be found during research; students will formulate their own answers supported with the information they have located.

Teaching Techniques

Teachers and library media specialists can use different techniques (such as worksheets, modeling, and individual conferences) to help students write appropriate research questions. A worksheet can provide an example thesis (or statement of purpose) and sample questions with space for students to write their own controlling statement and questions (see handouts 7.3 and 7.4).

If handout 7.4 is used and the students are pursuing high-level research, the teacher or library media specialist can modify the handout to specify the type of conclusion (hypothesis, prediction, solution, comparison / analogy, or judgment) required for a particular assignment. The appropriate general question presented earlier as a guide can be inserted to help students write their own interpretive question(s).

To model the question development process, the teacher or library media specialist can use a transparency of the worksheet. Students suggest questions for specific topics others in the class plan to research. Once the class has composed questions for a few topics, students can work individually to create their own research questions. They are not being asked to produce "right" questions but instead to think deeply about their topic and decide what they want to discover during research.

Because writing questions is crucial to thoughtful research, teachers should meet with students individually to check their work or help them complete a thesis (or statement of purpose) and questions that follow the three criteria: (1) the thesis and questions work together, (2) both are appropriate for the assigned level of research, and (3) questions cover every important aspect of the thesis.

A sample working session with Steven, who was featured at the beginning of this chapter, might proceed like this:

STEVEN (reading his statement of purpose): I plan to research the sport of boxing in the United States. I want to find out how dangerous the sport is and what can be done to make it safer.

TEACHER: OK. I think that statement of purpose will work well for your research. I see that you haven't written any questions.

S: I don't know what to write.

T: Let's start with this first category: overview information/statistics/definitions. What will you need to tell your classmates to give them background? Remember, most of them don't know nearly as much as you do about boxing.

S: Maybe they'll need a definition of boxing. [He scribbles a question with his pencil stub.]

T: What else will be important in this category?

S: How many people are into boxing?

T: Right! [Steven writes another question.] You've covered the first part of your statement of purpose—"I plan to research the sport of boxing in the United States." Let's move on to the next part.

S: [Reading] I want to find out if the sport is dangerous and....

T: Stop right there. Work on just that part now.

S: This is sort of a statistic, but maybe it could go here—How many boxers are injured yearly? And also, what types of injuries are most common?

T: Yes, I think it could go here as well as in the category above. [Steven writes furiously.] Remember that an interesting project is one that presents specific examples. People enjoy those.

S: Specific examples of injuries? OK, I'll write a question on that.

T: Now to the last part of your statement of purpose—"... what can be done to make it safer." Why do boxers wear those mouth protectors?

S: They have to.

T: Who says they have to?

S: OK, I get it: Who sets rules for boxing safety?

T: Good question!

S: Then, I need to find out for sure what the rules for safety are.

T: Right. Now you're ready for the last category.

S: I probably need to find out what changes people think should be made. [He constructs the question.]

T: If changes are made, do you think boxing will be less exciting?

S: Probably not, but....

T: Steven, I don't want you to answer that question now. I do think you should include something like that in your project, though. [Steven completes his questions.]

S: Can I tell everybody which new rules I think should be made?

T: Certainly! Just be sure your ideas come out of your research and be sure it's obvious that you're stating an opinion.

Steven's final research framework might be the following:

Statement of Purpose: I plan to research the sport of boxing in the United States. I want to find out how dangerous the sport is and what can be done to make it safer.

Overview Information/Statistics/Definitions
> What is boxing?
> How many people are involved with the sport as participants or as fans?

Background/Causes/Reasons
> How many boxers are injured yearly?
> What types of injuries are most common?
> What are some specific examples of injury?
> Who sets rules for boxing safety?
> What is being done now to prevent boxing injuries?

Effects/Solutions/Changes
> What other safety changes should be required?
> How would these changes affect the sport?

Classroom Management

The sample working session with Steven is not meant to suggest that students can always be easily led to develop useful questions, but one-on-one conferences will greatly increase the likelihood of success. These individual sessions, however, will also introduce a classroom management problem: What can the teacher and library media specialist do with all those students while focusing attention on one at a time?

Careful, cooperative planning can make this experience successful. The classroom teacher or the library media specialist can set up an "interview station" to check theses and questions. The free member of the team can supervise students moving on to the next step of the process, formulating a plan for their research.

Another possibility would be to teach the entire class some of the planning or source location techniques (chapters 8 and 9), then set up interview stations for both the classroom teacher and the library media specialist. Students, both those whose thesis/questions have been approved and those still awaiting a turn, could begin planning for research or finding sources, depending on the assignment.

With two or more adults, the checking can usually be completed within a typical period. If a few students still need interviews the next day, one member of the team can continue those while the other helps students with their research.

Still another way to handle the checking is to have the class visit the library media center for the overview step, then return to the classroom for thesis and question development/checking, planning, and perhaps some exercises to prepare for upcoming research. Students could, for example, complete some practice in taking notes.

An alternative to the teachers' checking each thesis/question sheet is peer evaluation. This will work particularly well if students have already helped each other with class projects and developed a trusting relationship.

CONTINUE USING QUESTIONS THROUGHOUT THE RESEARCH

The questions the students write at this point are not necessarily final; students should be willing to modify, discard, or add questions as dictated by their research. While researching, students should use their questions to decide whether the information is important or unimportant, relevant or irrelevant, an answer or a partial answer. Later, the questions (or the key words in them) will be used as a notetaking structure and as the basis for an outline.

COMPENSATION FOR THESE STEPS

Students gain critical thinking skills while developing a controlling idea and research questions. Because of time constraints on some assignments, however, teachers may choose to provide the thesis/question structure as a part of the assignment requirements (see handout 7.5). Questions should still range from the factual to the interpretive to encourage high levels of thought based on the research. Taking time when the unit is planned to develop such a research structure may also help teachers and library media specialists clarify the unit objectives and make the assignment more successful for the students.

REFLECTION POINT
Do the questions provide a foundation for my research?

The student should ask:

1. Do my questions go beyond simple, factual ones to interpretive or evaluative ones?

2. Do my interpretive or evaluative questions match the assigned level of research?

3. Do my questions cover every important aspect of my thesis or statement of purpose?

4. Do I have any unnecessary questions?

THESIS STATEMENTS vs. SIMPLE FACTS

A thesis statement is a controlling or unifying idea, a statement of the main theme of an entire paper or project. Some of the following sentences are thesis statements; others are simple facts.

Label each statement either "Thesis" or "Fact."

_____ 1. The development of the airplane contributed to the "shrinking world" phenomenon.

_____ 2. Che Guevara, the famous Cuban guerilla fighter, was reportedly killed on October 8, 1967.

_____ 3. The isolationist policy that the United States had followed after World War I was not pursued after World War II.

_____ 4. Great Britain and France were the leading members of the League of Nations.

_____ 5. The first major automobile race went from Paris to Marseilles.

_____ 6. The League of Nations failed because countries gradually recovered from their disillusionment with war after World War I; the United States refused to join; and the League had no power to enforce peace.

_____ 7. In 1956, the Gold Coast Assembly changed its name to Ghana after it was granted independence by Britain.

_____ 8. The concept of "teenagers" and teenage culture first developed in the 1950s due to the increasing economic independence of young people.

_____ 9. German propaganda during World War II was effective in creating popular support for Hitler and his policies.

_____ 10. Mahatma Gandhi used nonviolent, passive resistance in order to pressure Britain into granting independence to India.

(Information from Trevor Cairns. *The Twentieth Century*. London: Cambridge University Press, 1983.)

Suggested answers are on page 76.

Handout 7.1. Barbara K. Stripling and Judy M. Pitts, *Brainstorms and Blueprints: Teaching Library Research as a Thinking Process* (Englewood, Colo.: Libraries Unlimited, 1988).

Suggested answers for handout 7.1.

1. T
2. F
3. T
4. F
5. F
6. T
7. F
8. T
9. T
10. T

WRITING A THESIS STATEMENT

Read the statements below and write a thesis statement that could serve as a controlling idea for the facts presented.

1. Before the American Revolution, more than fifty thousand English convicts were shipped to the colonies.

2. After 1700, most of the servants who were imported to the colonies were convicts and vagrants; most were sent to the South.

3. The mortality rate among prisoners on board ship was extremely high—from 15 to 30 percent.

4. Between 35 and 50 percent of new indentured servants in the colonies died within five years of arrival.

5. Some of the convicts on nearly every passage were women. In the 1600s the women were traded for tobacco in Virginia; they became wives, or concubines, for the early settlers.

6. The colonies experienced a growing crime problem; colonists placed much of the blame on the fact that Britain was sending its overflow of prisoners to the colonies.

7. Plantation owners in Virginia were granted land according to the number of servants they purchased; no land was taken away if the servants happened to die after only a few months of service.

8. By 1700, laws were put into effect to prohibit the private burial of servants in order to curtail the landowners' practice of acquiring increasing numbers of servants (and thus more land) and then neglecting to provide proper care for them (because all that mattered for land grants was the initial purchase of the servants).

9. As a punishment for running away, servants were beaten and sentenced to additional indenture time (a multiple of the number of days they were away).

10. Small farmers and newly arrived settlers of the early 1700s received no benefits from convict labor; they opposed Britain's practice of sending prisoners to the colonies.

(Information from Frank Browning and John Gerassi. *The American Way of Crime*. New York: G. P. Putnam's Sons, 1980, pp. 87-94.)

Handout 7.2. Barbara K. Stripling and Judy M. Pitts, *Brainstorms and Blueprints: Teaching Library Research as a Thinking Process* (Englewood, Colo.: Libraries Unlimited, 1988).

STATEMENT OF PURPOSE AND RESEARCH QUESTIONS

STATEMENT OF PURPOSE: A simple statement of what you want to accomplish with your research.

Example: I plan to research the statistics and causes of teenage suicide and describe possible solutions.

QUESTIONS TO GUIDE RESEARCH:
1. *Overview Information/Statistics/Definitions*
   Example: What are important suicide statistics?

2. *Background/Causes/Reasons*
   Example: What causes teenagers to commit suicide?

3. *Effects/Solutions/Recommended Changes*
   Example: What could be done by adults to prevent teenage suicide?

* * *

YOUR STATEMENT OF PURPOSE:

QUESTIONS TO GUIDE YOUR RESEARCH: Try to write two questions in each category. Make sure your questions cover each part of your statement of purpose.

1. *Overview Information/Statistics/Definitions*

2. *Background/Causes/Reasons*

3. *Effects/Solutions/Recommended Changes*

Handout 7.3. Barbara K. Stripling and Judy M. Pitts, *Brainstorms and Blueprints: Teaching Library Research as a Thinking Process* (Englewood, Colo.: Libraries Unlimited, 1988).

THESIS STATEMENT AND RESEARCH QUESTIONS

THESIS STATEMENT: A formal statement of the main idea you want to present about a research subject.

Example: Current programs to prevent teenage suicide are ineffective because they focus on crisis intervention rather than on long-term stress management for teenagers.

QUESTIONS TO GUIDE RESEARCH:

1. *Overview Information/Statistics/Definitions*
   Example: What is the situation with teenage suicide at the present time?

2. *Background/Causes/Reasons*
   Example: What are the stressful factors in teenagers' lives?
   Example: How do current programs handle teenage suicide?

3. *Effects/Solutions/Recommended Changes*
   Example: What can adults do to relieve stress in teenagers' lives?
   Example: What effect do crisis intervention programs have on teenage suicide?

4. *Interpretation (Prediction)*
   Example: What will happen to teenage suicide rates if long-term stress management programs are established for teenagers?

* * *

YOUR THESIS STATEMENT:

QUESTIONS TO GUIDE YOUR RESEARCH: (Try to write two questions in each category.)

1. *Overview Information/Statistics/Definitions*

2. *Background/Causes/Reasons*

3. *Effects/Solutions/Recommended Changes found in the research*

4. *Interpretation of Information (hypothesis; prediction; solution; comparison/analogy; judgment)*

Handout 7.4. Barbara K. Stripling and Judy M. Pitts, *Brainstorms and Blueprints: Teaching Library Research as a Thinking Process* (Englewood, Colo.: Libraries Unlimited, 1988).

SOCIOLOGY—ETHNIC GROUPS IN AMERICA
STATEMENT OF PURPOSE AND RESEARCH QUESTIONS

Directions: Before beginning library research, you should always develop a *statement of purpose* and *research questions*. These items have two purposes: (1) They will give your research a goal and guide your group's members as you search for information; (2) They will provide a structure that will be useful when you plan your oral presentation.

     You may use the statement of purpose and questions provided below on this project.

STATEMENT OF PURPOSE: We plan to research the relationship of our assigned ethnic group to American society.

QUESTIONS TO GUIDE RESEARCH

1. What is the nature and what are the kinds of prejudice your group now faces or has faced in the recent past?

2. How has your group responded to the discrimination and prejudicial attitudes? How have dominant groups in American society responded to your minority group? How has your group's culture helped or hindered its adaptation to American life?

3. What problems/successes has your group encountered in the field of education?

4. What problems/successes has your group encountered in the job market? What are average incomes? What types of jobs are most commonly held by your group?

5. What familial patterns are evident within your group?

6. What important achievements have been accomplished by members of your group? Are there any particular "paths to success" used by many members of your group?

Handout 7.5. Barbara K. Stripling and Judy M. Pitts, *Brainstorms and Blueprints: Teaching Library Research as a Thinking Process* (Englewood, Colo.: Libraries Unlimited, 1988).

Chapter 8

STEP SIX
Plan for Research and Production

Stephanie rushed into the library as soon as the door was unlocked. "You remember that comparison-contrast project the American history classes worked on last week?" she asked breathlessly. "I need some pictures of fashions from the 1960s to finish my poster. Can you tell me where they are?"

The library media specialist, ever in a teaching mode, replied, "Where have you looked?"

"I haven't looked anywhere. Can't you just tell me where they are? I have to finish this poster by second hour." Stephanie desperately waved a crumpled piece of soiled poster board. A wandering black line divided the poster in half. On the right side Stephanie had pasted wrinkled cutouts of current fashions.

She and the library media specialist located the pictures, but the questions continued: "Do you have some glue I could use? Can I have a piece of white paper? Could I use that marker? The copier is making this picture too dark; can you fix it?"

Before first period, Stephanie's poster was complete, but it failed to communicate any research-based information. Instead, the poster revealed Stephanie's lack of planning.

Stephanie had made common mistakes. First, she had chosen the format she thought would be easiest to produce rather than the one suited to her topic, audience, and production skills. More importantly, she had failed to plan either her research or her production. Without a research plan, Stephanie had found a few facts but no visuals. Without a production plan, Stephanie had neither gathered the materials she needed nor allowed time for careful assembling.

Planning is an essential step for any thinking process. If the process is thinking-based *research*, students can plan best after they have focused on a narrow topic and set goals with their thesis statement and questions.

Planning is more than delineating step-by-step tasks. It can be a creative process that generates new approaches to the research problem and to the effective presentation of the results. Even the most creative planning, however, must be practical and include the steps to be performed, the amount of time needed for each step, the types of information to be gathered, and the production skills needed.

This planning step, like the reflection points throughout the research process, requires students to think about their research. Rather than looking backward, though, students look forward and devise a blueprint for upcoming research and production.

To complete this step of the research process, students must be able to:

1. Choose a presentation format which will be appropriate for the topic, audience, resources, and production facilities available.

2. Determine the types of information needed.

3. Plan research and production.

CHOOSE A PRESENTATION FORMAT

Choice of Format at This Point in the Research Process

This might seem early in the process to choose a format for the final project, but students like Stephanie need guidance to link their research firmly to their final presentation. The format decision shapes the types of information and resources the students must locate. Students can change the format later if information / resources cannot be located or new ideas arise.

Selection of Format by Teachers or Students

Students often do not have a choice about the format of their final product. When teachers or library media specialists plan a research assignment, they set the thought levels of the research and reaction, usually by assigning a specific final project.

The educators' specifying the final project offers some advantages. First, the expectations can be described on the assignment sheet. Standards for evaluation will thus be established early in the unit. Next, many students perform best if every step of the process and a timetable are laid out for them.

Last, because students are all working on similar projects, the teacher or library media specialist can plan lessons useful to the entire class and determine that appropriate resources will be available. For example, if students are required to make and laminate a poster, a "how to" lesson can be presented to the whole class.

Students may choose the format for their final project although this freedom may make them uneasy. Most have produced "term papers," but have not designed an advertising campaign or videotaped a talk show segment. Even a creative written project, such as the presentation of a historical event from two points of view, may intimidate students firmly entrenched in the term paper rut.

Students gain several skills by choosing a format. They make their own decisions about their presentation, basing them on their assessment of the topic, audience, and resources available. Depending on their choice of format, students may acquire new writing, presentation, or audiovisual production skills as they present their information in the most effective manner possible.

These new skills provide an enticing critical-thinking by-product: Students learn to analyze many types of messages for effectiveness and bias.

Considerations in Choosing a Format

Students choosing a presentation format must use critical thinking to connect their topic to a format. They must ask: How can this topic best be presented? Perhaps it requires visualization. Students describing for their classmates the construction of a Renaissance cathedral will find the task easier with visuals. Other students dealing with local pollution problems will discover that slides, posters, picture displays, charts, and graphs emphasize their points. Other topics, such as the impact of the Beatles on popular music, may require the use of sound.

Students must also consider the strengths and limitations of the various formats. Some, such as video, effectively combine motion, sound, and special effects but are difficult to produce. Others, such as slides or photo displays, are easier to create but offer only still images. Some formats use color. Others, such as thermal transparencies, offer excellent black-line, detail reproduction of images. Some media, such as transparencies, can be directly controlled by the presenter. Others, such as videotapes, have built-in pacing once completed. Imaginative combinations (for example slides with recordings, posters with a speech, or transparencies as a background for a skit) are possible.

Another consideration when choosing a presentation format is the potential audience. Who will be receiving the information—classmates, the teacher, a panel of experts, a community group? What can be done to increase communication with them? Do they need to see as well as hear information, read as well as watch? If audience members lack motivation to learn, would a creative approach stimulate communication? For example, in addition to combining the verbal cathedral information with visuals, the student might arrange for an "interview" with a cathedral architect or stonemason. The researcher concerned with the local pollution problem might present to his audience a "letter" written by a town resident fifty years in the future.

In considering their format choice, students must recognize the types of audiovisuals they can produce, given their school environment. Some schools may offer sophisticated production facilities; others may have nothing more than a countertop with poster board and a few stencils.

Students' expertise in producing audiovisual materials may also be a factor. Some media require training and previous experience or professional assistance for successful production. Others can be created and used by novices.

Many students will have to be taught necessary production skills. Educators may decide where to place these skills within the research process. While students should make a format decision at this point, some teachers and library media specialists will prefer to present actual media production skills later, probably at step ten of the process, create and present final product. Others will provide an overview of the skills early so that students' production planning can continue simultaneously with the research.

Production expenses—both in time and money—must also be considered. Some productions, such as transparencies, can be completed in a few minutes once planning decisions have been made. Others, such as slides with a synchronized tape, require extensive planning and preparation time.

DETERMINE TYPES OF INFORMATION NEEDED

Before making any final format decision, students must predict the types of information they will need for their project. If they will be creating a dramatization, they will require personal information rather than statistics. They may also want pictures of fashions during the relevant time period to guide costuming. If they will be compiling a scrapbook for a historical person, students must gather facts about the subject's life and times, and pictures of important events and people.

The following list summarizes the types of information that might be available. Students should select the types most appropriate for their own research project.

Type of Information Needed

General overview information

Supporting information:
[examples, causes, effects, comparisons/contrasts, proof, arguments]

Not extremely current

More current

Specific, detailed information:
[definitions, statistics]

Predictions/conclusions/hypotheses

Biographical information

Primary source information

Illustrations/pictures/photographs

The sample assignments below, taken from the REACTS taxonomy, are paired with predictions students might make about the types of information needed:

Level 2 Assignment: Cut out newspaper ads that would have interested a historical figure you have researched. Explain their importance to the historical figure.

Predicted Information Needs: Personal information (e.g., personality, likes, dislikes, hobbies, interests) of the subject. Newspapers and magazines which can be clipped.

Level 3 Assignment: Construct a collage depicting the social pressures influencing your subject.

Predicted Information Needs: Facts about the subject's relationship to society. Newspapers and magazines which can be clipped or photographs and drawings which can be copied and cut apart.

Level 4 Assignment: Determine as a movie producer whether to make a film of a historical event and justify the decision.

Predicted Information Needs: A chronology of events; information about the people and settings involved.

Level 5 Assignment: Design and produce a television commercial or whole advertising campaign which presents your research results to the class.

Predicted Information Needs: Information about the topic which can be visualized and easily summarized. Pictures, charts, maps, or other visuals which can be adapted for video photography or print layout.

Level 6 Assignment: Create a new country and describe the change in the balance of power in the world.

Predicted Information Needs: Information about international relations, the balance of power, and changes in that balance of power. Maps on which to place the new country. Perhaps color pictures which can be turned into slides of the new country.

PLAN RESEARCH AND PRODUCTION

After the format of the final project has been selected and the information needs identified, students can plan their research and production. Planning is an essential step of research which most adults perform automatically and most students have never heard of. Planning compels the students to examine the entire project and direct their energies toward the final goal—an effective presentation of well-researched information.

Planning also helps students focus on the information rather than the production. The guiding principle of any type of media production/presentation is to *communicate information*. Media items should be used only to enhance the message.

A final advantage to this planning step is a time management one. Some students have trouble completing a lengthy project, not because they are lazy, but because they do not know how to divide a large task into workable parts. Many students do not impose deadlines on themselves for each step of a project; they expect to pull the whole project together right before the teacher's deadline.

Students can use a research planning sheet to lead them through a five-step planning strategy (see handouts 8.1 and 8.2).

Step 1: Set Goal

If the students have followed the research process to this point, they have already set their research goals by formulating their thesis statement and writing questions. Their production goal was set when they were assigned or chose the format for their final product.

Step 2: Break the Research and Production into Workable Parts

A basic planning strategy is to break a problem into parts that can be accomplished in short periods of time. The research process itself, because it is performed step-by-step, divides the project.

Teachers and library media specialists can help students break each step of the research process into subsections by requiring students to set a daily goal or giving the goal to them. Students may be told, "By the end of class today, you should have found an additional source and have taken some notes from it."

Step 3: Place the Parts in Sequence

The steps of the research process are arranged in a logical order, but additional sequencing within the steps can tailor them to individual learning styles. Some students prefer to take notes on one research question at a time, working through every source for each question. Other students are more comfortable finding information in each source on all their research questions before moving to another source.

The sequencing for audiovisual production is especially important. Students must perform each step of the process in order. If students are producing a videotape, they must develop a storyboard before writing the script.

Step 4: Decide What Resources Are Needed

Students have already predicted what types of information they will be seeking. At this step, they need to consider what types of resources will provide that information for both their research and production.

The table below shows a variety of information needs. Each is paired with the types of sources which would supply the best information.

Type of Information Needed	Best Source(s)
General overview information	reference books
Supporting information: [examples, causes, effects, comparisons/contrasts, proof, arguments]	
Not extremely current	regular books
More current	magazine and newspaper articles
Specific, detailed information: [definitions, statistics]	reference books
	magazine and newspaper articles
Predictions/conclusions/ hypotheses	regular books
	magazine articles
Biographical information	reference books
	magazine articles
Primary source information	regular books reference books
Illustrations/pictures/photographs	all of the above

Students should also determine that all necessary production resources will be available at the proper time. If something vital (such as a video camera) will not be available, students should change their production goals or their schedule.

Step 5: Set Completion Dates for Each Workable Segment

Students have trouble pacing themselves to complete their research projects on time without some in-process deadlines. Teachers or library media specialists may assign these deadline dates, or preferably, students may choose their own completion dates.

Students should keep their plan in mind throughout their research and production, constantly assessing their progress. If they notice a problem with their research or with their plan, they should re-evaluate and change their approach. If students cannot locate prices of common items in colonial America (and the library media specialist cannot either), then they should change their plan of producing a chart comparing colonial American prices with current costs.

COMPENSATION FOR THIS STEP

Teachers and library media specialists can compensate for this step by assigning the research format and determining a research and production plan. The teacher or library media specialist decides on the presentation format, breaks the project into workable parts, and assigns deadlines for each task. Beginning researchers may need this structure. Students should still be made aware of the planning process and of in-process deadlines.

A good intermediate step is for teachers to build choices into the assignment. By using the suggested projects from the REACTS taxonomy in chapter 2, teachers and library media specialists can design several assignments from which the students may choose. Whatever the individual choices, all class members will encounter a variety of formats and thus widen their own options for future reactions to research.

REFLECTION POINT
Is the research / production plan workable?

The student should ask:

1. Does my chosen presentation format fit my topic, audience, and available resources?

2. Have I determined what types of information and sources I need?

3. Will the information and production resources be available for me to complete my final project?

4. Do I have a workable timetable for completing various phases of my research and production?

5. Am I prepared or can I get the training to produce necessary media items?

RESEARCH PLANNING SHEET

Topic:

Goal/Thesis:

Research Questions:

Description of final product:

Types of information needed and probable sources:
    Information   *Source*

Types of production materials needed:

Sequence and schedule for research:
    Research Task   *Deadline*

Sequence and schedule for production:
    Production Task   *Deadline*

Final Presentation Date:

Handout 8.1. Barbara K. Stripling and Judy M. Pitts, *Brainstorms and Blueprints: Teaching Library Research as a Thinking Process* (Englewood, Colo.: Libraries Unlimited, 1988).

SAMPLE RESEARCH PLANNING SHEET

Topic:
Changes in fashion following the stock market crash of 1929.

Goal/Thesis:
The dramatic changes in fashions which occurred following the 1929 stock market crash were directly related to economic and social conditions in the country.

Research Questions:
What was America like—socially, economically, politically—before the 1929 crash? What were fashions like from 1920-29? What was the country like—socially, economically, politically—following the 1929 crash? What were fashions like from 1930-35? How did social, economic, and political events affect fashion?

Description of final product:
An oral report accompanied by visuals (posters and transparencies) and music.

Types of information needed and probable sources:

Information	*Source*
Social, economic, political information for 1920s and 1930s	Reference, regular books
Fashion information including illustrations	Regular books
Music from the 1920s and 1930s	Record collection

Types of production materials needed:

Materials	*Source*
Thermal transparencies	School
Poster Board	Me
Glue	Me
Markers	Me

Sequence and schedule for research:

Research Task	*Deadline*
Locate 3 sources	January 18
Take notes/find pictures, source 1	January 20
Take notes/find pictures, source 2	January 22
Take notes/find pictures, source 3	January 26
Locate reference source/take notes	January 28
Choose music	January 29
Draw conclusions/create final outline	February 1

Sequence and schedule for production:

Production Task	*Deadline*
Write script and turn in for teacher comment	February 5
Revise	February 10
Create transparencies	February 12
Create posters	February 16
Transfer music to cassette	February 17
Rehearse	February 18

Final Presentation Date: February 19

Handout 8.2. Barbara K. Stripling and Judy M. Pitts, *Brainstorms and Blueprints: Teaching Library Research as a Thinking Process* (Englewood, Colo.: Libraries Unlimited, 1988).

Chapter 9

STEP SEVEN
Find / Analyze / Evaluate Sources

Geoffrey slammed the card catalog drawer and muttered to himself as he reached for his tattered folders, three thick texts, and a Piers Anthony paperback.

"What's the matter Geoffrey? Do you need some help?" the library media specialist inquired.

"No. I'm going to the university library tonight. This library doesn't have anything."

Before Geoffrey could stalk away, the library media specialist asked, "What are you working on?"

"I have to do a background paper to support my science fair project on solar energy, and there's nothing here I can use." He waved toward the card catalog.

"What did you look under?"

"Solar energy. You only have two books, and I have them checked out."

Geoffrey was correct; only two books were listed under "solar energy." But Geoffrey had not transferred his scientific thought processes to library research. Worse, he was planning to use a more complex academic library with the same poor search techniques.

Luckily, the library media specialist encountered him and gently offered assistance. Together they located five more books, several magazine articles, and four pamphlets with information on solar energy.

Many students' locational skills consist of a mechanical, two-step process: search and find. If searching does not immediately lead to finding, students abandon the task; if sources are located, they often prove to be inappropriate.

By adding critical-thinking (*selection*) skills to their locational (*collection*) skills, students can build a search strategy to find appropriate information for any research task. Students will move from "This library doesn't have anything," to "What else can I look under to find more information?" and ultimately to self-sufficiency in locating and using information.

The thoughtful search strategy involves sequential or simultaneous performance of several steps: plan, search, find, analyze, evaluate.

To complete this step of the research process, students must be able to:

1. Plan an effective search strategy.

2. Search for information using appropriate sources and search techniques.

3. Examine each possible source quickly (check the table of contents, index, subheadings, picture captions, appendices).

4. Analyze each probable source according to scope, depth of treatment, arrangement, and special features.

5. Use primary sources.

6. Evaluate the reliability of each source.

PLAN AN EFFECTIVE SEARCH STRATEGY

During the previous step of the research process, students developed an overall research plan. They identified the type of information they needed, as well as the probable best source(s) for each.

Before students begin to seek those sources, they can develop an effective search strategy by identifying the place to begin looking for each type of source and by expanding their list of subject headings.

Identifying the Place to Begin Search for Each Type of Source

The following chart will show students the relationship between *what* they need and *where* to begin their search:

Type of Information Needed	Best Source(s)	Place to Begin
General overview information	reference books	card catalog, reference collection
Supporting information: [examples, causes, effects, comparisons/contrasts, proof, arguments]		
Not extremely current	regular books	card catalog
More current	magazine and newspaper articles	magazine index, database
Specific, detailed information: [definitions, statistics]	reference books	card catalog, reference collection
	magazine and newspaper articles	magazine index, database
Predictions/conclusions/hypotheses	regular books	card catalog
	magazine articles	magazine index, database
Biographical information	reference books	card catalog, reference collection
	magazine articles	magazine index, database
Primary source information	regular books, reference books	card catalog, reference collection
Illustrations/pictures/photographs	all of the above	card catalog, reference collection, magazine index

Expanding List of Subject Headings

No matter where students start to look for answers to their questions, a list of alternate subject headings will be helpful. Students began such a list in step two of the research process when they brainstormed broader, narrower, and related terms before finding an overview (see handout 5.1).

As the search for information expands throughout the library, the subject heading list must also grow. Students can use several tools to *find* alternate subject headings: cross references, tracings, subject heading sources such as *Sears List of Subject Headings*, and database thesauri.

The first tool, cross references, will be familiar to most students, although they may not recognize these as subject-heading aids. Cross references appear in most library sources — indexes (both within books and in separate publications such as magazine indexes), the card catalog, and encyclopedia articles. Students can record on their subject-headings sheets the cross references (both "see" and "see also") that they find.

Tracings (subject headings listed on the bottom of main entry catalog cards) are a second subject-heading source. These headings will be particularly useful in the card catalog but may also work elsewhere.

A third tool for finding subject headings is a source such as *Sears List of Subject Headings*. Students should realize that librarians do not originate subject headings for the card catalog; instead, standardized headings are published for library referral. The source of subject headings (usually *Sears* in school libraries and *Library of Congress Subject Headings* in academic and large public libraries) should be available for student use.

Another subject-heading source, database thesauri, should be on hand if the library has access to national databases.

The teaching team can explain the subtleties of different subject-heading sources or can expect students to learn to use them from the explanation included with each book.

The number of acceptable subject headings for each research subject will vary according to the resources available and the research subject itself. A little thought, combined with the use of *Sears* and the cross references in the *Readers' Guide*, results in the following list for Geoffrey. He will have to pick the headings specific to the aspects of solar energy that he is researching.

Architecture, Domestic
Automobiles, Experimental
Barns and stables — Heating and ventilation
Electric batteries
Electricity
Energy
Energy resources
Engines
Greenhouses
Heat storage
Heating
Heliostats
Kennels
Photovoltaic power generation
Power
Refrigerators
Renewable energy resources
Solar batteries
Solar cells
Solar collectors
Solar energy

Solar energy industry
Solar engines
Solar heating
Solar homes
Solar houses
Solar pumps
Solar radiation
Solar rooms
Solar water heaters
Sun

SEARCH FOR INFORMATION USING APPROPRIATE SOURCES AND SEARCH TECHNIQUES

Searching for Regular Books

Armed with their list of subject headings, students use the card catalog (or perhaps a computer catalog) to locate books in the regular collection. Ironically, the card catalog may be more of an obstacle than an aid. Alphabetization can be word by word or letter by letter. Punctuation (such as dashes, parentheses, and commas) in the top line of the card also influences the filing. Finally, some cards are filed chronologically (U.S. - POLITICS AND GOVERNMENT - 1933-1945 would be filed before U.S. - POLITICS AND GOVERNMENT - 1971-1975).

Students using more than one library for their research will find that card catalogs are to some extent idiosyncratic to each institution. Researchers who are having trouble with a card catalog should try the following steps:

1. Find the place where they think the cards *should* be, then thumb through an inch of cards before and after the area.

2. Look up other ways the same words might be filed (as one word instead of two; as plural instead of singular).

3. Realize that in a large catalog, a misunderstanding of that institution's filing rules can make a difference of literally several drawers.

4. Ask for help. Make the request specific. "I've been trying to find (*subject*) and can't seem to locate it under the heading (*subject heading*). Can you find it or suggest some other subject headings I might check?"

Once students have call numbers, they still must locate the items on the shelves. Codes within the call number may designate special materials (audiovisual items or periodicals) or special shelving locations (for oversize or reference books). Finding the particular source, therefore, requires familiarity with the library or a willingness to ask for directions.

Many students approach locating sources in the narrowest sense: They write down a call number for a specific book and look for that one book. Unfortunately, that book may be out of place, checked out, or missing. These students declare that the library has nothing on their topic.

Teachers and library media specialists can counter this narrow approach by teaching a *browsing process for the regular collection.*

1. Find all appropriate call numbers and titles in the card catalog. Many subjects will appear in more than one Dewey area.

2. Go to those shelves and look for specific titles.

3. Browse in those areas for any other appropriate title.

4. Examine any likely book.

5. If sufficient sources are not located, return to the card catalog and look up broader subject headings. Repeat the browsing process, checking for chapters or sections within the books. (Information on dreams can be found in books on psychology, the brain, and sleep.)

6. If necessary, browse the first ten numbers of each relevant Dewey area where the more general books will be located. (Information on the French Revolution will be in the 944s. Additional facts may appear in general history books located from 900 to 909.)

Teachers and library media specialists can model the browsing process for individual students who need help. Using judgment about the frustration level of the student, the teacher or library media specialist can work with the student through each step, offering advice and encouragement. Often the students stagger away from the shelves (which only a few minutes earlier contained nothing on their topics), carrying more information than they dreamed they could find.

Searching for Reference Books

All libraries have a reference collection, but few students understand what it is; thus, they do not find the valuable overview and supporting information readily available there.

Students will benefit more from instruction on the use of the reference collection as a whole than from a lesson on specific reference sources. When appropriate, however, specific source lessons may be included within a unit. (Most library media specialists would rather teach three classes of thirty students each to use *Contemporary Literary Criticism* than give ninety individual lessons.)

An introduction to the reference collection can begin with a definition: "A reference book is a book (on one subject or many subjects) that is designed to be searched for specific items or sections of information. It is *not* designed to be read straight through." By comparing books on the same subject, students will see that a book from the regular collection will have chapters built one upon another, while a reference book will be in another format such as a dictionary or encyclopedia. The user can look up a specific term or concept, read the usually brief information, and go on to another source.

Students will probably be familiar with the different types and functions of reference books. Dictionaries usually provide short, succinct definitions. Encyclopedias are best for general information and overviews. Almanacs and handbooks specialize in statistics and other brief facts. Atlases supply maps.

These general types of reference books can be found throughout a reference collection. If a short definition of a term in botany is needed, students can use a dictionary of biology or botany. If a basic understanding of the Teapot Dome scandal is required, students can choose an encyclopedia of history. While the editors of reference books do not always apply the labels (dictionary, encyclopedia, handbook) accurately to reflect the contents of the book, students can usually make a prediction of a book's contents.

Finding information on a particular topic within the reference collection is confusing because the card catalog does not always help. Reference books contain too many subjects for each to be listed in the card catalog. A sports encyclopedia will include archery, badminton, bagatell, fishing, football, golf, horseshoes, parachuting; there will not be a direct card catalog reference from each sport to the book.

The best way to locate information in reference books is to use a *browsing process for the reference collection.*

1. Use the card catalog and broad subject headings to find call numbers for the regular collection.

2. Use the same numbers in reference. (Most students do not realize that if they have been using the number 796 to locate information about football in the regular collection, the same number will work in the reference collection.)

3. Scan the titles in that Dewey range (the 700s), a simple task in most reference collections. (The library may not own an entire reference book on a particular topic like football; students may have to select a general sports book.)

4. Examine any likely book.

5. If necessary, check the 000s in reference, since that area contains books with many different subjects (like the general encyclopedias).

Searching for Magazine Articles

Unless students have access to electronic databases, they will probably use a print index to locate magazine articles on their research topic. If the teaching team decides that students need to review how to read the entries in available indexes, worksheets can be developed or are available in many English textbooks. An alternative to presenting such a lesson is to make available instructions (purchased or developed in-house) for using the magazine index.

Learning to read an individual entry in a magazine index is only one step in locating periodical information. More useful would be a *browsing process for a magazine index.*

1. Choose the magazine index volumes with the dates most appropriate for the subject. (This time-related aspect of the topic should have been discovered in the overview.)

2. Use the previously developed list of subject headings, subheadings, and additional cross references in the index to find information. Try several subject headings in each index.

3. Scan the titles of the articles to select those that seem most helpful.

4. Look at the name of the magazine for each article selected. Choose those that most closely resemble the orientation of the research. (Students performing high-level research can select magazines which offer in-depth articles.) Refer to posted lists to be sure the library has that magazine available.

5. Look at the number of pages. (One seven-page article will contain more comprehensive information than seven one-page articles.)

Searching for Newspaper Articles

Students may have access to newspaper articles in several formats, including microfilm, microfiche, and electronic database.

Newspapers on microfilm are generally limited to a single title per film, as in *The New York Times* on microfilm, and access may be through an index specific for that newspaper.

Programs like NewsBank (NewsBank, Inc., 58 Pine Street, New Canaan, CT 06840) and Facts on File (Facts on File, Inc., 460 Park Avenue South, New York, NY 10016) offer excerpts, abstracts, or complete-text articles from newspapers throughout the country. Depending on the source, these articles or excerpts are available on microfiche or in looseleaf and bound volumes. Each source includes subject indexing; the same subject headings and browsing process successful in a magazine index will work in an index to newspaper articles.

Searching Electronic Databases

National, electronic databases are available in some school libraries across the country. By using these sophisticated information tools, students can find citations to documents, magazines, and newspapers; locate abstracts of articles; and even read full texts of wire service news stories and some magazine and encyclopedia articles.

In some school systems, students are being prepared for database searching in the elementary grades. They gain an understanding of electronically stored information by creating a small database. After performing simple research in print sources, they record their facts on a database program and make the results available to others in the class.

Another alternative, elementary through senior high, is to use prepared database programs on countries of the world, states of the United States, biomes, and other subjects. These databases offer students a chance to retrieve information for their classes while they learn to manipulate data with a computer.

Database users must be subject-heading experts. An understanding of subject-heading concepts for the library's print resources will transfer readily to databases. In addition, set theory is important, and teachers who display Venn diagrams to demonstrate subject combinations give students a head start on database use (see chapter 5).

Once students have some basic understanding of electronic information, they can use various programs to simulate online searches. For example, the ERIC system offers a floppy-disk, offline search simulation at a nominal cost. (For information write Information Resources Publications, 030 Huntington Hall, Syracuse University, Syracuse, NY 13210 or call 315-423-3640.) CD-ROM (Compact

Disc-Read Only Memory) sources, such as the *Academic American Encyclopedia* (available for less than half the cost of the print version), can be used to provide valuable, up-to-date information and to demonstrate search routines.

Search strategies for online databases differ from those for CD-ROM sources. Online searches are performed against a clock; users must plan extensively if the search is to be successful and economical. CD-ROM searchers, on the other hand, can take time to browse entries. In some cases, searches of backfiles can now be made on CD-ROM; the search strategy can then be saved and typed in automatically for efficient online searches of the most current data.

Some library media specialists require that students do considerable preliminary work in the library's print sources before searching online. A form can help students develop their search strategy (see handout 9.1). The student's subject headings sheet is attached to this search form, and teachers check note cards or sheets before a student begins an electronic search.

Other library media specialists do not require students to have searched the print collection extensively, asking only for well-thought-out thesis statements and research questions, along with subject-heading lists that have been checked against the database thesaurus. These library media specialists believe that students will use available print resources to construct their theses and questions and will follow their online search with additional print research.

Online searches can be performed by students; however, an adult with database experience should be near to offer assistance with searching and logging on and off. An instant log-off feature within the communications software will allow quick escape if a search strategy proves unworkable.

Searching the Vertical File

While card catalogs differ somewhat from library to library, vertical files differ dramatically. They may even have different names such as "information file" or "pamphlet file." Whatever its name, some file of current and ephemeral material exists in nearly every library.

Often these files contain valuable research material that cannot be located in books or periodicals, but students will have to be reminded to check for this information. Cross-references in the card catalog can lead students to specific topics in the vertical file.

ANALYZE EACH POSSIBLE SOURCE

Students may have trouble determining the usefulness of the sources they locate. For a quick, at-the-bookshelf judgment, they can examine the table of contents, index, subheadings, picture captions, and appendices.

A "scavenger hunt" can be used to teach these quick-judgment analysis skills. The students' objective in this activity is to locate background facts for a particular unit such as a study of communications. A Dewey clue sheet can guide their hunt for useful books throughout the library (see handout 9.2).

For more detailed analysis, students can examine the following four aspects of their sources:

Scope: subjects covered; geographical and chronological limits.
      Students can check the title and subtitle, preface, introduction, foreword, table of contents, and inside cover for this information.

Arrangement: alphabetical; topical; chronological; comparative.

Students believe that an alphabetically arranged book is the easiest to use. Alphabetical books, however, often do not include an index which makes the use of correct subject headings vital. Students must use cross references, which may be located within, between, or at the end of articles.

Depth of Treatment: length of entries.

This information will be useful if students are seeking a specific type of information. Definitions will not be helpful if the student needs statistics, examples, or an overview.

Special Features: illustrations; unusual indexes; charts; graphs; tables; bibliographies; appendices; glossaries.

Special features (especially prevalent in reference books) increase the value of a resource. Unless students are made aware of the features, they often miss the useful information included there.

Students can learn to analyze resources through a unit on examining reference books. They draw slips of paper (each of which lists a particular reference book or set), find their source, and examine it as the class discusses the four aspects described above. Much of the analysis process can be drawn from students if they are asked questions like: "How can you determine the scope of a book?" or "What are some special features *your* book includes?" Once they have analyzed their own book, students present the in-depth information to their classmates. After this activity, students will be able to analyze any new sources they locate.

USE PRIMARY SOURCES

Advanced researchers in secondary school should begin to seek and use primary sources when appropriate. Primary sources are documents or visuals which were created by a participant or observer for communication of an idea, not for research. They are in their original form, often without interpretation or explanation; this means that students must draw their own conclusions, an important critical thinking skill. Primary sources offer an immediate picture of events. Often they reveal information not found elsewhere and serve as an excellent source of compelling quotes for a research project. Primary sources may include letters, speeches, diaries, wills, interviews, government documents, photographs, and videos.

Students beginning to use primary sources should be aware of some problems. The sources are often difficult to read, with language that is complex, archaic, or full of jargon. The document represents one point in time, with no explanation of preceding or following events. No study helps such as explanatory footnotes appear in the original text. Primary sources are often biased, one-sided, and emotional because of a limited perspective. Even photographs, which would seem a true picture of a subject, can be taken from an angle meant to hide rather than reveal the facts.

Students using primary sources may need some study hints to decipher the information. Reading slowly and carefully and making good use of a dictionary should be the first steps. Other helpful activities include reading background material (secondary sources) before tackling the primary source, using "self-questioning" techniques to clarify understanding, being aware of bias and emotionalism, reading the document several times, and using copies so that notes can be made on the document.

An effective way to make students familiar with primary sources is for the teaching team to locate several sample documents. Each student can be assigned one source to study before general class discussion of primary sources.

If a fairly broad definition is used, primary sources can be found in a typical school library media center. The H. W. Wilson series, *Representative Speeches*, offers transcripts of speeches on current topics. *Historic Documents* (Congressional Quarterly) publishes a yearly volume of speeches, treaties, court decisions, and laws. Oral history, such as *Bloods* (Random House, 1984) or Al Santoli's *Everything We Had* (Random House, 1981), both books about the Vietnam conflict, presents history in the words of those who lived it. Original video footage of historic events is often included in instructional video series, and study prints offer still photographs of historic moments.

EVALUATE THE RELIABILITY OF EACH SOURCE

Once students have located their sources, they need to evaluate them by considering the qualifications of the writer, the reputation of the publisher, the general accuracy of the source, and the point of view.

Qualifications of the Writer

Students can often find out about the author from the blurbs on the cover, within the book, or at the end of a magazine article. Students evaluating two books about genetics may discover that one is by a physician and the other by a free-lance writer. Both books can prove useful. The physician's book may be more authoritative; the writer's may be easier to understand.

Reputation of the Publisher

Secondary school researchers may have difficulty assessing the reputation of publishers, but they should be aware that publishers often specialize in different areas; this specialization may influence the orientation of the source. Students who become aware of the publishers in their fields of interest can start to build a stock of evaluative opinions. Students may also consult the teacher or library media specialist for additional information about publishers.

Accuracy

Researchers should determine whether or not their sources are likely to be accurate. An extensive bibliography and articles or chapters well documented with footnotes usually indicate careful verification of the facts. In addition, students can check the copyright date, realizing that an old source may be inaccurate.

Point of View

The point of view of a source is influenced by its purpose—to entertain, inform, or educate. Students quickly grasp the difference and the relative usefulness for research when shown specific examples.

Some sources, such as news magazines, reflect a specific political or social point of view. Students can often determine a magazine's or book's point of view by reading editorials or prefatory material. They may also require direct information from their library media specialist who will find this an opportune time to explain that a library's objective is to purchase a balanced collection, although each source will not necessarily present all points of view.

COMPENSATION FOR THIS STEP

Teachers and library media specialists cannot compensate entirely for this step of the research process, but they can simplify it when necessary. The most complete compensation would be providing students with a bibliography of useful sources. In addition, the materials themselves can be pulled from the shelves and placed on reserve to ensure that each student will have access to adequate information.

An alternative to the bibliography, which allows slightly more student involvement, is providing students with a pathfinder. A pathfinder can work students through a search process while it leads them to specific books in the library (call numbers are given) (see handout 9.3).

Another way to simplify finding sources is for library media specialists to prepare a subject-heading sheet for students (see handout 9.4). Students will still be expected to analyze and evaluate the materials they find.

REFLECTION POINT
Are my sources usable and adequate?

The student should ask:

1. Have I found an acceptable number and variety of sources (books, reference materials, periodicals, vertical file)?

2. Is each source reliable?

3. Have I found a balance of points of view?

Conference Date _____

Search Date _____

DATABASE SEARCH REQUEST

NAME:

DESCRIPTION OF SUBJECT/PROJECT:

TEACHER:

SOURCES ALREADY USED

    OVERVIEW SOURCE:

    OTHER SOURCES:

RESEARCH QUESTIONS WHICH LACK SUFFICIENT INFORMATION:

DATABASE TO BE SEARCHED:

CONCEPTS (Key words or phrases that best describe your topic.) Circle the correct connector (and/or) between your concepts.

A		B		C
	and		and	
	or		or	
_____		_____		_____

Synonyms and
Computer Format

Bring to the conference: SUBJECT HEADINGS SHEET and NOTES

Handout 9.1. Barbara K. Stripling and Judy M. Pitts, *Brainstorms and Blueprints: Teaching Library Research as a Thinking Process* (Englewood, Colo.: Libraries Unlimited, 1988).

LANGUAGE / COMMUNICATION—DEWEY DECIMAL CLUE SHEET

001.5	Communication; Sign language
001.6	Data processing; Computers
070	Journalism; Publishing; Newspapers
137	Graphology (handwriting analysis)
153.6	Verbal and nonverbal communication (including body language)
301	Society and language
302.2	Mass media
305.7 - 305.8	Language groups; Racial, ethnic, national groups
324.7 - 324.9	Use of media in politics
325.4 - 325.9	Immigration
384	Communication systems (e.g., telegraphy, radio, television)
398	Folklore including riddles, rhymes, and folk and fairy tales
400	Language
410	Linguistics
411	Written language
417	Dialects
419	Indian sign language; Deaf sign language
420	English and Anglo-Saxon language
422	Word origins
427	Slang; Dialects (e.g., Black English)
428	Standard English usage
497	Maya hieroglyphs
591.5	Animal communication
602	Trademarks and symbols
649	Child development
652	Written communication
659	Advertising
780	Music
792.3	Pantomimes
793.7	Word games
796.03	Language of sports
907	Oral history
917.3	American place names
929.4	Personal names
929.6	Heraldry

Handout 9.2. Barbara K. Stripling and Judy M. Pitts, *Brainstorms and Blueprints: Teaching Library Research as a Thinking Process* (Englewood, Colo.: Libraries Unlimited, 1988).

SOCIAL PROBLEMS/FAMILY RELATIONS RESEARCH GUIDE

For *overview information* on your social problems/family relations research topic, please check the following reference books (which are listed in the card catalog only under broad headings like PSYCHOLOGY or SOCIOLOGY not under the narrower topic ideas):

R/150/Enc	Encyclopedic Dictionary of Psychology
R/150.3/Enc	Encyclopedia of Psychology
R/158/Ins	Instant Relief: The Encyclopedia of Self-Help
R/174.2/Enc	Encyclopedia of Bioethics
R/300.3/Int	International Encyclopedia of the Social Sciences
R/301.3/Enc	Encyclopedia of Sociology

For *supporting information* (examples, causes, effects, comparisons, proof, arguments), you can probably use both books and magazine articles. We suggest you look under the following subject headings to find your material in the *card catalog* and the *Readers' Guide*. (CC = Card Catalog; RG = *Readers' Guide*) Be sure to check the magazine lists to see which magazines we take.

Divorce
CC: Marriage; Family; Domestic relations; Social problems; Social change; Parent and child; Children; Women
RG: Divorce; Alimony; Remarriage; Support (Domestic relations); Children of divorced parents; Divorced fathers; Divorced mothers; Divorcees; Marriage; Family

Teenage Pregnancy
CC: Adolescence; Adolescent psychology; Pregnancy, adolescent; Pregnancy; Sex education; Sex; Sexual ethics; Unmarried mothers; Parent and child
RG: Teenage pregnancy; Youth—Sexual behavior; Sex education; Pregnancy

Child Abuse
CC: Sexually abused children; Child abuse; Children
RG: Child abuse; Child molesting; Shaken child syndrome; Children—Crimes against; Crime; Child welfare

Single Parenting
CC: Marriage; Family; Parent and child; Children; Social problems; Parenting; Women
RG: Single fathers; Single mothers; Single parent families; Divorced fathers; Divorced mothers; Divorcees; Widows; Widowers; Children of divorced parents

Adoption
CC: Adoption; Child welfare; Parenting; Children; Women
RG: Adoption and adopted children; National Adoption Exchange; Parent and child; Parent-child relationship; Parents; Children; Child welfare

Foster Home Care
    CC: Foster home care; Children—Care and hygiene; Children
    RG: Foster home care; Social work with youth; Children—Care and hygiene; Child welfare; Children—Law; Children, Homeless; Cluster homes (Juvenile housing); Parent and child

Battered Spouses
    CC: Family; Family violence; Wife abuse; Battered wives; Women
    RG: Wife abuse; Family violence; Violence

Effects of Alcohol and/or Drug Abuse in Families
    CC: Alcoholism; Adolescence; Children; Alcohol; Alcoholics; Drugs; Drug abuse; Social problems; Women
    RG: Alcohol; Alcoholics and alcoholism; Alcoholics' families; Alcohol and women; Alcohol and youth; Drug abuse; Drugs and children; Drugs and women; Drugs and youth

For *supporting information from the reference collection,* try the same call numbers that worked in the regular collection. If the identical numbers do not work, browse more widely in that area in reference.
    Example: In the 362s in reference, you will find:
    R/362.2/Enc   The Encyclopedia of Alcoholism
    R/362.2/OBr   The Encyclopedia of Drug Abuse
    R/362.7/You   Youth Problems

For *specific laws and statistics,* check the following reference books:
R/317.3/Uni   Statistical Abstract of the United States
R/317.3/Uni   U/S: A Statistical Portrait of the American People
R/348.736/Gui   The Guide to American Law
R/349.73/Fam   Family Legal Guide
R/364.03/Enc   Encyclopedia of Crime and Justice

Handout 9.3. Barbara K. Stripling and Judy M. Pitts, *Brainstorms and Blueprints: Teaching Library Research as a Thinking Process* (Englewood, Colo.: Libraries Unlimited, 1988).

SOCIOLOGY RESEARCH UNIT
Ethnic, Racial, and Minority Groups in America

Readers' Guide Subject Headings

General Information
Children of immigrants
Culture conflict
Discrimination
Discrimination in education
Discrimination in employment
Discrimination in housing
Discrimination in sports
Equal pay for equal work
Housing—Desegregation
Immigrants
Immigration and emigration
Language and languages
Minorities
Public schools—Desegregation
Race Discrimination
Race Relations

Native American Indians
Indians of North America
Indians of North America—Culture
Indians of North America—Women

Black Americans
Black athletes
Black children
Black entrepreneurs
Black family
Black leadership
Black organizations
Black students
Black women
Black women—Employment
Black youth
Black—
Blacks
Blacks—Employment
Blacks—Housing
Blacks—Segregation
Ku Klux Klan

Spanish Speaking Americans
Cuban Americans
Cubans in the United States
Hispanic Americans
Mexican Americans
Mexicans in the United States
Puerto Ricans in the United States
Refugees, Cuban

European Americans
Anti-Semitism
Europeans in the United States

German Americans
Germans in the United States
Irish Americans
Irish in the United States
Italian Americans
Italians in the United States
Jewish women
Jews
Jews—United States
Neo-Nazis

Asian Americans
Asian Americans
Asians in the United States
Chinese Americans
Chinese in the United States
Japanese Americans
Japanese in the United States
Vietnamese in the United States

Elderly and Women
Aged
Aged—
Aged—Economic conditions
Aged—Employment
Aged—Housing
Aged—Legal status, laws, etc.
Aged—Medical care
Aged—Mistreatment
Aging
Black women
Black women—Employment
Feminism
Jewish women
Married women—Employment
Old age
Sex discrimination
Sex discrimination in education
Sex discrimination in language
Women
Women athletes
Women bankers
Women clergy
Women entrepreneurs
Women executives
Women immigrants
Women—
Women—Attitudes
Women—Crimes against
Women—Economic conditions
Women—Employment
Women—Equal rights
Women—Occupations
Women—Social conditions

Handout 9.4. Barbara K. Stripling and Judy M. Pitts, *Brainstorms and Blueprints: Teaching Library Research as a Thinking Process* (Englewood, Colo.: Libraries Unlimited, 1988).

Chapter 10

STEP EIGHT
Evaluate Evidence / Take Notes / Compile Bibliography

Jennifer industriously scribbled notes onto bright pink 3-by-5-inch cards. "Teenage suicide is an ever-growing problem in American society today. Psychologists say...." She filled each card with the embellished printing that was her trademark—circles above each "i"; curly tails on most capitals; large, rounded letters.

At the end of a paragraph in her book, Jennifer sat back, smiling at her burgeoning stack of note cards. Then she spied the pile of untouched sources mocking her from the edge of the table, and her smile twisted into a grimace. "I'd better hurry. I'm only on page fifteen of my first source, and I haven't even looked at these other books."

The library media specialist's voice interrupted her reverie. "Class, you should be taking notes from your third source today. I will be coming around to help those of you who are having trouble."

Jennifer slammed shut the book she had been using and grabbed another one off her stack. She turned to page one and started copying with a flourish. She could hear Ken and Dave at the next table rehashing last Friday's dance. She'd wanted to go, but she'd had to visit her aunt in Kansas City. Boring!

"Did you see Beth dancing with Lucas? I didn't know they were even friends." Ken's wistful expression displayed his own feelings about Beth.

Jennifer listened attentively to their conversation as she continued copying from her second source. At this rate, she could probably get thirty cards done today. Scribbling note cards furiously, she thought, "Ken obviously likes Beth. I wonder who Dave likes."

The library media specialist briefly paused at Jennifer's table, saw her stack of completed note cards, and went on to help Ken and Dave whose enthusiastic gestures indicated they were talking about something other than research.

Jennifer has a more serious research problem than Ken's and Dave's tendency to gossip rather than work. At least Ken and Dave know they are not researching; Jennifer thinks she is. She measures progress by her stack of note cards and so far has done about two inches of research; but Jennifer, like so many other students, is paying no attention to what she is writing on those cards.

Jennifer *has* performed several steps of the research process correctly—she has picked a topic that interests her; she has written questions and a thesis statement; and she has found four sources. Unfortunately, she has also missed the main point of research—thinking about the topic and the information.

To complete this step of the research process, students must be able to:

1. Focus on the main ideas of the research questions.

2. Locate relevant information within a source.

3. Use a "thought-full" notetaking cycle.

4. Analyze the information to determine if it answers research questions.

5. Evaluate the information.

6. Take appropriate notes to avoid plagiarism.

7. Use note cards or learning-log note form efficiently and effectively.

8. Use correct bibliographic form as specified by the teacher.

FOCUS ON THE MAIN IDEAS OF THE RESEARCH QUESTIONS

Jonathan is writing a research paper about special academic requirements for student athletes. His thesis statement is: "Special academic requirements for high school athletes unfairly discriminate against them; the requirements should be changed to the same ones that any student has to follow in order to stay in school."

Jonathan had no trouble writing research questions because he is interested in his subject:

1. What are academic requirements for high school athletes in my state and in surrounding states?

2. What is the background behind these requirements?

3. Why were these requirements put into effect?

4. What has been the effect of these requirements?

5. What changes in the requirements are being suggested for the future?

6. How might those changes be put into effect?

7. What effect might those changes have on the athletes and on the school sports programs?

When Jonathan was ready to take notes, he discovered a problem. He knew his thesis and questions were good—Mrs. Fitzgerald, the library media specialist, had said so. But he was overwhelmed by the amount of information; he had no idea where to start taking notes.

Jonathan stared at his sources without lifting a pen for two days before the library media specialist discovered him in a study carrel. Mrs. Fitzgerald led Jonathan through the first step for taking notes—figuring out the main focus for the research and the key concept in each research question.

First she had him write one phrase that represented the main idea in his thesis statement—academics and athletics. Then for each question he listed one key word or phrase.

1. Present academic requirements

2. Background

3. Why requirements?

4. Effect now

5. Suggested changes

6. How to make changes

7. Effect of changes

Jonathan could see from his key words that his paper would have two areas of emphasis—the situation now and the situation in the future. He broke his questions into two categories along those lines (between questions four and five). After he had identified key words, Jonathan could keep his major ideas in mind more easily as he took notes.

Some students will not respond well to listing key words; instead, they might design a graphic representation to help them focus their research. In *Teaching for the Two-Sided Mind*, Linda Verlee Williams offers several visualizing alternatives which can be adapted and modeled for students at this stage of the notetaking process. Jonathan might enclose his thesis phrase in a circle or rectangle and list his key words on rays emanating from that center.

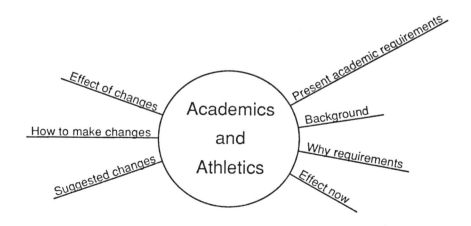

Students who experiment with visual representations will see new relationships among ideas. Patterns will develop. Visual representation may also cause students to change any questions which no longer fit the pattern. To establish a parallel with the questions he asked about the present system, Jonathan may decide to eliminate his second question about background and change his sixth question from "How might these changes be put into effect?" to "Why might these changes be necessary?"

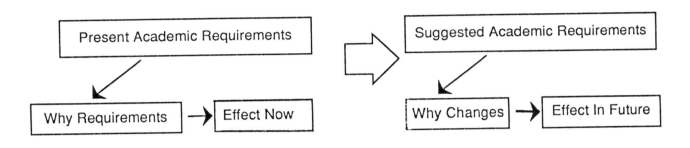

LOCATE RELEVANT INFORMATION WITHIN A SOURCE

Students often are manipulated *by* information, rather than being manipulators *of* information. They take notes for the amount of time they have, starting on page one of the sources and copying whatever they find, never realizing that they can choose to take notes on only the best information.

Students who have worked carefully through the research process have already determined the types of information they need. At this step of the process, students focus on locating information *within* sources by using the techniques described below.

Using the Table of Contents

For a broad vision of a book and for an idea about where to start browsing for information, students may check the table of contents (using the broad subject headings from their list). Topics important enough to be covered by an entire chapter are often listed only in the table of contents. "Greek art" may not even be included in an art book index if a whole chapter is devoted to the subject.

Using the Index

The index gives specific page references for narrow subject headings. Students should first check the sections with the most continuous pages.

Using Contextual Clues

Contextual clues will help students locate information within the text of a book or article. A variety of clues (chapter subtitles; boxed information; special charts, graphs, or illustrations with explanatory headings; items featured in color or graphically accented) identify important material.

Using Skimming and Scanning Techniques

Once students have used tables of contents, indexes, and contextual clues to locate sections of useful information, they can skim the material for a sense of the main ideas included.

Skimming is rapid, selective reading. Students let their eyes glide over the text until something seems pertinent. They can usually read paragraph topic sentences for main ideas, then skim the rest of the paragraph.

If students are looking for specific information (such as a statistic or a name), they can use scanning techniques. Students visualize the information, then let their eyes zigzag across the page for that detail.

If Jennifer had used all the techniques for locating information within a source before taking notes on teenage suicide, she would never have started notetaking in all of her sources at page one. Instead, she would have obtained a sense of the major points in each source and pinpointed particular pages for later, more careful reading and notetaking.

USE A "THOUGHT-FULL" NOTETAKING CYCLE

If the notetaking process is full of thought, the steps form a cycle which includes questioning, analyzing, and evaluating information.

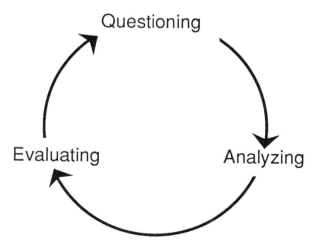

The cycle should be in place for all but the lowest level of research. At the second and third levels, students will use simple analyzing to select the best answers to their questions. At higher levels, students will use more sophisticated questioning, analyzing, and evaluating skills.

ANALYZE THE INFORMATION TO DETERMINE IF IT ANSWERS RESEARCH QUESTIONS

The main criterion for students to use in analyzing the information they have found is: *"Does the information answer one of my research questions?"* Relevant material defines, explains, illustrates, or serves as an example of a topic. Students trying to decide if material is relevant can check their key idea diagram to see where each piece of information fits into the research scheme. If the information does not fit and yet is important, students can write a new question and change their research scheme.

Another assessment students can make is: *"Does this information further my understanding?"* Students should take notes on new supporting ideas, but may be able to skip examples and illustrations if they have already recorded similar ones. Unfortunately, many students are not adept at rejecting information. If they record their main and supporting ideas on their diagram, they will be able to spot duplicated information.

Students should consider a final analysis question: *"Is my information complete?"* A glance at the diagram will help students target any main point which needs further support.

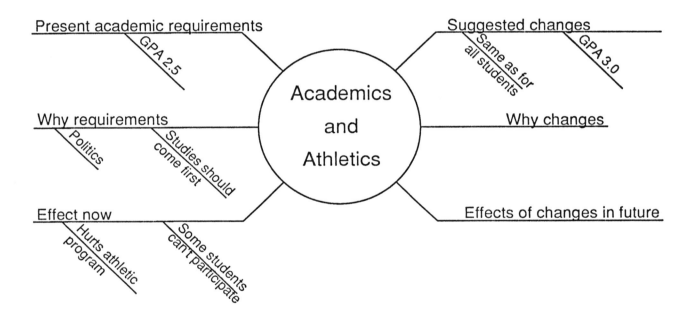

EVALUATE THE INFORMATION

Students performing high-level research should evaluate as well as analyze information. Evaluation involves forming a judgment based on a number of criteria. Students can be introduced to these criteria gradually; they should not be expected to apply all of them to each research project.

Practice on specific evaluation skills (such as those described below) can be given in small assignments until students are familiar enough with the skills to apply them in a larger context. Several sources offer exercises on specific skills, including many books of the Opposing Viewpoints series from Greenhaven Press and *Critical Thinking (A and B)* in the Scholastic Social Studies Skills series from Scholastic, Inc.

Determining the Accuracy of the Facts by Comparing Sources

Students can be alerted to the potential problem of inaccurate information and advised to compare several sources. They will be more likely to discover factual mistakes in newspapers and magazines than in books.

Recognizing Statements That Are Facts and Those That Are Opinions or Value Claims

Many secondary students have difficulty differentiating facts from opinions and value statements. Facts are provable, but the proof may not always be stated or obvious.

Recognizing provable statements is usually easy in scholarly materials because footnotes, in-text references, and bibliographies lead readers to the writer's proof. Not all library materials are scholarly, though, and students need to recognize some clues that signal facts, opinions, or values.

Facts: most active verbs; present and past tenses of "to be" verbs (is, was, has been); statistics; specific details that can be proven true or false.

Opinions: most subjunctive verbs (could, might, would); verbs expressing opinion (believe, think, assume); qualifiers (probably, maybe, almost, supposed, perhaps); hypothetical situations (if...); predictions of future events (will, ought to); adjective qualifiers (fine, unnecessary, scandalous).

Values: judgments on a continuum from good to bad; comparisons (sweetest, nicer, happier).

Teachers and library media specialists can develop a fact/opinion practice unit using editorials and letters to the editor. A combination of individual student practice and class discussion focusing on the clues above will raise students' awareness levels.

Students may use facts, opinions, and value claims in their research projects as long as each is properly handled. Unique facts should be footnoted; opinions and value claims should be attributed to their authors in the text, and students should cite the authors' qualifications whenever possible ("In the opinion of Dr. Joe Samuelson, director of laboratory research,...").

Distinguishing Bias from Reason

To detect bias, students must understand that an author's point of view (which is defined as a personal frame of reference including attitudes and values) can affect factual presentation. If the author's point of view does not intrude on the accuracy and reliability of the writing, no research problems occur.

Students can learn to recognize point of view by writing about a situation from various points of view. If the class is studying child labor laws, students can write about a day in the textile mills from the point of view of a child laborer and then from the point of view of the textile mill owner. This activity will help students realize that writers filter facts through their own experiences; the resulting points of view influence writers' perceptions of events, people, and issues.

Once students understand point of view (frame of reference), they can begin to recognize bias — a closed frame of reference based on emotion, rather than reason. Biased writers have closed their minds to evidence that contradicts their point of view; consequently, they present a one-sided picture of their subject.

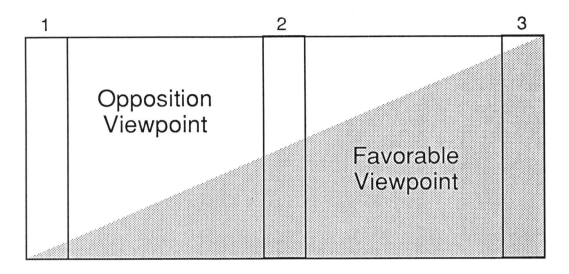

Writer 1 — presents all facts in opposition to an issue with barely a mention of arguments in favor.

Writer 2 — presents a balanced viewpoint.

Writer 3 — presents all facts in favor of an issue with barely a mention of opposing arguments.

Biased language is full of emotionally charged, loaded words that make the reader or listener respond emotionally rather than rationally. A unit focusing on propaganda techniques can provide valuable practice in detecting bias.

Recognizing Fallacies in Arguments and Reasoning

When students are performing high-level research, they must recognize inaccurate or distorted arguments such as those described below.

Proof by Selected Instances

Instead of offering evidence, the author selects one or two examples to prove a point. Example: The parole system should be abolished. One prisoner was paroled after serving only ten years of his twenty-five-year sentence for armed robbery. The very next week, he killed a convenience store clerk in a robbery attempt.

Unstated Assumptions

The author bases the major ideas of the writing on assumptions that are never made clear and may be wrong. Example: In order to reduce the number of traffic accidents, no one should be permitted to drive until the age of eighteen. (Assumptions: Sixteen-year-olds are worse drivers than eighteen-year-olds; sixteen- and seventeen-year-olds cause many traffic accidents.)

Deceptive Arguments

The author "proves" points by using an analogy that does not hold up or by stating the case as an either/or situation, when in fact a variety of alternatives may exist. Example of analogy: In tight economic times, schools should react as any business by practicing strict cost-cutting measures and reducing programs accordingly. (Analogy: Schools are businesses.) Example of either/or: White collar criminals should be given suspended sentences rather than be sentenced to prison if they reimburse for damages.

Oversimplification

The author makes complex events or situations appear simple or easy to solve. Example: People are depressed because they are lonely. The best treatment is for them to participate in social situations more often.

Appeal to Authority/Tradition

The author claims that something is true because some authority says it is or because it has always been that way. The quoted authority may not be an expert in the field in question. Example: American children are more militant in their attitudes today than ever before. This trend has been pointed out by Franklin Popover, president of the multi-million-dollar business, Popover Toys.

Bandwagon

The author claims that a statement is true because everyone thinks so, or everyone is doing it. Example: All Americans know that politics are dirty.

Television or magazine advertising can be used to teach students to recognize fallacies in reasoning. Students study videotaped or print advertisements and then produce their own ads. Each ad should include at least two fallacies of reasoning which other students in the class identify.

TAKE APPROPRIATE NOTES TO AVOID PLAGIARISM

The four most common types of notes are citation, summary, paraphrase, and quotation. Each type is useful and appropriate in specific notetaking instances.

The *citation* is the exact copying of specific facts, definitions, and statistics which must be precise in the final project. If exactly the same information is found in more than one source, it probably will not have to be footnoted, although students should maintain a record of the source and page number in case they decide to footnote later. An example of a citation note might be: "Children who watch an average amount of television see about 300 murders per year."

In *summary* notes, students read a large section of the text for the overall meaning or main ideas and summarize the information in one to two sentences. This type of note is used when students are beginning their research and are encountering general, explanatory material. Unless the explanatory material represents an author's original theory or an unusual approach to a subject, summary notes generally will not be footnoted in the final paper.

When students *paraphrase*, they work with smaller sections of text, putting the ideas in their own words. This type of note is most appropriate for supporting information, biographical information, predictions, hypotheses, and conclusions. Paraphrasing is difficult for most students because they can rarely think of words that express the meaning as well as the original. Paraphrased notes are the most common; they also lead most easily to plagiarism. They may or may not need to be footnoted, depending on the general availability of the information.

The *quotation* note should be reserved for one- or two-sentence statements that are particularly effective in proving a point or revealing an attitude. Quotation notes, which are especially appropriate for primary sources, must be footnoted in the final paper. The quotations should be used only as proof or backup for statements that the students made in their own words; students should not use the texts of quotations to make points for them.

To review, the notes most commonly taken on the major types of research information are as follows:

Type of Information	*Type of Note*
General explanatory material	Summary
Supporting information:	Paraphrase
Examples	
Causes	
Effects	
Comparisons/Contrasts	
Proof	
Arguments	
Specific details:	Citation
Definitions	
Statistics	
Predictions/conclusions/ hypotheses	Paraphrase
Biographical information	Paraphrase
Primary source information	Quotation

Notetaking practice should be required of students prior to a major research project. Once all students have read the same magazine article, they list five to ten important words from the text and write brief summary notes around each. These can be checked by the teacher or library media specialist who may also wish to assign specific segments for paraphrase practice. During class discussion, students can identify details which require citation or quotation.

The teacher or library media specialist should react to each student's work individually. A few students easily develop notetaking skills; others require much practice and guidance. The end result — useful notes and reduced chances of plagiarism — will make both students' and teachers' efforts worthwhile.

The seriousness of plagiarizing should be emphasized to students of all ages. The policies for dealing with it must be spelled out and consistent throughout the school.

Even at the third grade, fact-finding-research level, students should not be allowed to copy from a source. When they can copy at the elementary level, students do not understand the sudden stigma against it in junior or senior high.

If a paper is the final product of the research, the teacher and library media specialist can head off plagiarism by checking notes to catch copying early. Notes and a rough draft should be turned in with the final product for every research project, whether the final project is written, visual or oral.

Alternative assignments to the research paper can help teachers and library media specialists control plagiarism (see chapter 2 for ideas that can be adapted). The more creativity the final project requires, the less likely are students to plagiarize.

USE NOTE CARDS OR LEARNING-LOG NOTE FORM EFFICIENTLY AND EFFECTIVELY

Taking Notes Efficiently

In order to take notes efficiently, students need to set up a system that works for them. No matter what the system, the research questions must form the structure for notetaking. Students must also maintain their working bibliography, entering and assigning a number to every source they use.

The notes can be set up efficiently in either of two ways — on sheets of paper or on note cards. If the students use paper, they set up a sheet for each question, with the question written at the top. Every note taken on each sheet should answer that question. The source number and page for each note is written in the left margin.

If students use note cards, they can match their cards to their questions with the key words. They write the key word (as well as the page and source number) at the top of each card. Some students may prefer to color code their questions and cards. Whatever the system, the link between research questions and notes must be strong.

No matter how much experience the students have had in notetaking, a few reminders might help them: (1) write one idea per note (if using paper, separate the ideas with space), (2) do not copy, (3) limit quotations to one or two sentences and be sure to use quotation marks, (4) take notes only on those items that answer the questions, (5) indicate the page, source number, and question/key idea for each note, and (6) include as much specific detail as possible to make the research come alive.

Some students will want to make copies of their source materials and underline relevant sections instead of taking notes. While this practice might seem efficient, students will have difficulty later sorting and categorizing the information they underlined. In addition, most students will find it difficult to avoid plagiarism unless they write notes in their own words and create their projects from those notes.

Taking Notes Effectively

Effective notetaking means that students have gone beyond copying whatever they find to questioning, analyzing, and evaluating information before they write it down. It also means that students *react* to the notes in a thoughtful way, bringing their own background, knowledge, and point of view to the subject.

Reactions should be written next to the notes. If students are using notetaking sheets, a "learning log" format will allow these reactions.

Question: _____

Source/Pg	Notes	Reactions

If students are using note cards, they should select 4-by-6-inch cards and divide the card vertically, one half for notes and the other for reactions.

The reactions can vary according to the information and the goals of the students; they can be questioning, reasoning, or emotional reactions. Example reactions for a research project on pit bulls to use as samples during class presentation of the learning-log concept are listed below.

1. Questioning reactions:
    "Why?"; "Does this match my other sources?"; "How does this fit with my overall ideas?"; "What can be done about this problem?"; "What does this mean?"; "Why are no statistics included to prove this?"

    Example: "Is this one of the reasons that pit bulls have become so popular?"

2. Reasoning reactions:
    Generalizing—Drawing from the evidence to make a general statement about the problem or situation.

    Example: "It seems that pit bull attacks are becoming enough of a problem that some kind of regulation will have to result."

    Comparing—Making a comparison with information previously located or with knowledge that the student already has.

    Example: "Pit bulls are as violent as Dobermans used to be."

    Patterning—Trying to find a pattern for the research and discover where this piece of information fits into the pattern.

    Example: "This is a *cause* of increasing pit bull violence."

Evaluating—Judging whether the idea is good or bad, useful or not useful.

Example: "Requiring that all pit bulls be registered is a good idea. It might stop some of the dangerous cross breeding that is going on."

Inferring—Making a decision about what the information is really saying.

Example: "Owners who train their pit bulls to attack must have something against society."

Concluding—Making a conclusion about the overall idea of the subject.

Example: "Ownership of pit bulls is increasing, but pit bulls are a symptom of a problem in society, not a cause."

Predicting—Making a prediction about the status of the situation in the future.

Example: "I think the increasing ownership of pit bulls in ghetto areas will mean decreasing use of handguns in those areas."

3. Emotional reactions:
    Agreeing/disagreeing; judging value on a personal level.

    Example: "I don't agree with pit bull owners that the dogs are good-natured unless trained to be vicious. I think they are dangerous."

Reactions are difficult because most students do not feel confident in questioning their sources, making connections not specified in the materials, or including their own opinions. Yet, students who react to their notes will have thought through their research before they create a final project. The result will be a sophisticated combination of researched material and the student's own research-based conclusions.

The "thought-full" notetaking process, then, includes thought both in taking notes and in reacting to the notes. The notetaking cycle involves the student in questioning, analyzing, and evaluating the information in the sources. The reacting cycle asks the students to extend the information in their notes with their own questions, reasons, and feelings.

The notetaking and reacting cycles can be depicted as follows:

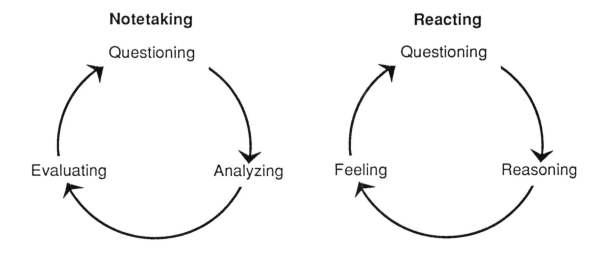

USE CORRECT BIBLIOGRAPHIC FORM AS SPECIFIED BY THE TEACHER

Students are often confused about what bibliographic information to write down for each source. Several acceptable bibliographic styles exist; the "correct" form depends upon the choice of the teacher who can devise a worksheet to help students list all necessary information for each source (see handout 10.1). This source sheet is especially useful to beginning researchers. Later, they can put all the information into the correct format.

Even if style books with sample bibliographies (for example, the *MLA Handbook*) are made available, most students will find it easier to use a sample bibliography of simple entries prepared by their teacher or library media specialist.

Every teacher in a school does not need to adopt the same bibliographic style. Students can adapt, as they will have to if they go on to college. Every teacher should make clear what style is considered correct for that teacher's projects. Various teachers' samples can be posted in the library media center for student reference.

COMPENSATION FOR THIS STEP

Students must perform this step of the research process; however, their level of evaluation may vary. Students performing low-level research may analyze their information only to see which question it answers. As the students move to higher levels of the research taxonomy, they should work on more of the evaluative skills included in this step.

Teachers cannot think for the students, nor should they allow students to take notes without thinking. By requiring thoughtful structures (such as visualizations of theses and questions or notetaking diagrams), teachers can encourage careful consideration of researched information. Students will see the pattern of their information more clearly, which will help them later when they create an outline and final project.

Students should not be expected to perform every part of this step on any research project. Working on one or two aspects of evaluation per project would gradually build the students' evaluative skills and lead them to higher levels of the research taxonomy.

REFLECTION POINT
Is my research complete?

The student should ask:

1. Have I found enough accurate information to answer all my questions?

2. Have I taken the notes in my own words?

3. Are my notes complete enough to be used without going back to the sources?

4. Is each note keyed to the question it answers and properly credited with source and page number?

5. Have I begun to identify relationships and reacted thoughtfully to my notes?

6. Is my bibliographic information complete?

BIBLIOGRAPHY WORKSHEET

Encyclopedia

Author of article
Article Title
Name of Encyclopedia
Place of Publication
Publishing Company
Copyright Date
Volume
Pages

Book

Author
Title
Place of Publication
Publishing Company
Copyright Date
Pages

Magazine Article

Author
Article Title
Magazine Title
Magazine Date
Pages

List below all necessary information.

Source 1

Source 2

Source 3

Source 4

Handout 10.1. Barbara K. Stripling and Judy M. Pitts, *Brainstorms and Blueprints: Teaching Library Research as a Thinking Process* (Englewood, Colo.: Libraries Unlimited, 1988).

Chapter 11

STEP NINE
Establish Conclusions / Organize Information into an Outline

When the bell signaled the beginning of lunch, most students grabbed their stacks of notebooks, texts, and library materials and hurried from the media center. Fred was an exception. When he picked up his tattered English folder, it literally fell apart, scattering research notes, old themes, and unfinished worksheets.

"Fred, you're going to be late to lunch," the library media specialist commented. "Let me help you get all that back together."

They gathered the papers, and Fred stuffed them randomly into his huge, blue duffel bag where they joined an assortment of other papers, gym shoes, several paperback novels, a few comic books, and a sack lunch.

Eyeing the disorganization, the library media specialist smiled, "That's an interesting filing system. I guess most of these papers are your notes for your research project. Your outline is due tomorrow, isn't it? Have you reached any conclusions about diabetes?"

"I don't know. I've got all my notes in here somewhere, but I haven't had time to think about them. I don't know why I have to do a stupid outline anyway."

"Fred, why don't you come in right after school? I'll give you some quick tips for organizing your information and coming to some conclusions. And bring your blue filing cabinet."

Fred grinned at her reference to his chaotic duffel bag. "Thanks, Miss Stengler, I could use some help."

Fred's organizational and decision-making problems are typical. During the teenage years, students find that teachers expect high levels of thought and organization in academic assignments. At the same time, a lack of training in those skills and the disorientation and emotionalism of adolescence undermine students' efforts to produce thoughtful, organized work.

Students told to "draw conclusions" or "prepare an outline" often do not do so, not out of defiance, but out of inexperience. When they are confronted with large quantities of complex, factual information (like their research notes), they must be *taught* to manipulate the information both mentally to establish some conclusions and physically to create an outline.

The mental and physical reorganization of information can be simultaneous or sequential. Some students need to establish their major conclusions before beginning their outline; others use the outline to discover information patterns and possible conclusions.

To complete this step of the research process, students must be able to:

1. Find or draw conclusions based on the evidence.

    —Follow a process for reaching a conclusion.

    —Identify and infer relationships among data.

    —Identify possible conclusions.

    —Choose conclusions best supported by evidence.

    —Establish conclusions at assigned levels of the research taxonomy.

2. Develop an outline for the final product.

    —Understand the necessity for outlines.

    —Organize with a traditional outline or visualize with a nontraditional outline.

    —Use the outline.

FIND OR DRAW CONCLUSIONS BASED ON THE EVIDENCE

Following a Process for Reaching a Conclusion

If students have progressed through the thoughtful research process to this point, they are ready to reach conclusions about their topic. For the low levels of research, they simply find someone else's conclusions and support them with evidence. At the high levels of research, students draw their own conclusions based on evidence.

Students can follow a process for reaching research conclusions:

1. Review research questions and thesis statement.

2. Go back over the notes, looking at both the evidence and the thoughtful reactions. Find the major problems, issues, or questions that arose during the research.

3. Work with the major ideas and the supporting information to see how all the ideas are related. Is one idea the cause of another? Were there changes in the ideas over time?

4. Identify reasonable conclusions based on the evidence and relationships discovered.

5. Test the conclusions by finding the evidence to support each one.

6. Choose the best conclusions.

The following sections explain the skills necessary for establishing conclusions, with examples drawn from a *Time* magazine article about Asian-American students who excel academically (Brand, 1987).

Identifying or Inferring Relationships among Data

Up to this point, students have been thinking about and reacting to individual pieces of evidence. When students draw conclusions, however, they must look at the ways their evidence fits together, how the pieces are related to each other. Relationships they might discover include: patterns; similarities and differences; cause and effect; part versus whole; and change over time.

Patterns

Students might identify patterns in the evidence—certain people behaving in a predictable way; cycles with events or attitudes disappearing and reappearing; societal values changing from one end of the spectrum to the other.

Example: Asian-American students have established a pattern of academic excellence, especially in math and science. In addition, there seems to be a pattern of Asian-American parents making sacrifices to foster academic success by their children.

Similarities and Differences

Students can look for similarities and differences between types of people, situations, events, issues or whatever they have been researching. The comparisons may be stated in the evidence or they may be inferred.

Example: Asian-American children are similar to early-1900s European immigrant children in their ability and willingness to take advantage of the opportunities offered in America. Their opportunities are different, however. Asian-American children now more often have the opportunity to attend school while earlier immigrant children had to work or combine work with school.

Cause and Effect

Students may discover the causes or effects of certain situations.

Example: Because Asian-American parents actively support their children's school efforts, the children are more likely to succeed academically and regard school as important than are their Caucasian counterparts.

Part versus Whole

Students can recognize the main ideas contained in their evidence and differentiate those from the supporting ideas.

Example: Discrimination against Asian-Americans is being practiced (main idea). Not only are they being harassed in some secondary schools, especially in the larger cities (supporting idea), but some of the better universities are apparently establishing quotas for the admission of Asian-American students (supporting idea).

Change over Time

With some subjects, students can identify a change over time. If conditions have gradually changed for better or worse, or if a person's behavior has altered, students should identify that change through the evidence they have collected.

Example: As Asian-American families blend more into American society, they are putting less emphasis on some of the traditional Asian values that led to high academic achievement. As a result, when Asian-American families have been in this country for several generations, their children no longer tend to stand out as high achievers at school.

Identifying Possible Conclusions Based on the Evidence Collected and Relationships Discovered

Throughout the research process, the students have practiced divergent thinking through brainstorming, questioning, and challenging. Conclusions, on the other hand, represent convergent thinking, or integrating ideas. Students can reach conclusions with any of several methods—by recognizing or making a summary, generalization, hypothesis, prediction, solution, analogy, or judgment.

Summary

Summaries of evidence are the most common, but least creative, conclusions. Most student papers rely on this method, as do many books and magazine articles.

Example: Asian-American students excel academically for a variety of sociological reasons.

Generalization

A generalization goes beyond a summary to include other people or situations that are not covered in the evidence. Students must decide if the evidence is strong enough to warrant a generalization that covers all similar situations.

Example: Immigrant children perform better academically than children born in the United States because they learn to work harder to achieve success.

Hypothesis

Students who conclude with a hypothesis understand their subject well enough to predict what would happen *if* a different situation were in effect.

Example: If Caucasian families placed as much emphasis on education as Asian-American families, their children would do as well academically as Asian-Americans.

Prediction

Students may conclude with a prediction, based on the evidence they have collected about the past and present situation.

Example: Asian-American students will predominate in American high-tech management positions within the next ten years.

Solution

If students have been researching a problem, they may suggest a solution in their conclusion.

Example: Forbidding top universities from imposing Asian-American quotas will relieve much of the pressure on Asian-American students to outstudy their schoolmates.

Analogy

Students may make their research subject clearer or more meaningful by developing an analogy.

Example: The situation of many first-generation Asian-American families is like that of many Jewish families who emigrated from Europe during or after World War II. Both were lucky to escape from a life-threatening situation; both were willing to exert extraordinary effort to make a life in a new country; both remained haunted by their narrow escape.

Judgment

Students may conclude with a final judgment of their subject, based on the evidence they have collected.

Example: It is wrong for any institution of learning to discriminate based on race. Even if quotas sometimes have the positive effect of boosting the number of ethnic students accepted, quotas should be abolished because they are discriminatory.

Choosing the Conclusions Best Supported by the Evidence

For most research subjects, several types of conclusions might be appropriate. Students should choose a conclusion best supported by the evidence they collected, which in turn was influenced by the thesis statement and research questions.

Students should include a summary conclusion for most research projects. At the high levels of research, students should add one of the other types of conclusions (generalization, hypothesis, prediction, solution, analogy, judgment).

Unless the conclusion is a summary, it is more than a restatement of the thesis. The thesis statement spells out the problem to be investigated; the conclusion states the solution or final judgment. A thesis statement on Asian-American children might read: Asian-American children excel academically because they study hard, they value achievement, and their parents give them strong support.

If students find evidence that Asian-Americans excel in math and science, that they are entering technological fields and advancing rapidly, that their parents are willing to sacrifice their own careers for their children's advancement, and that the Asian-Americans have a culturally based drive to achieve, then the previously cited prediction would be the most appropriate conclusion: Asian-American students will predominate in high-tech management positions within the next ten years.

Establishing Conclusions at Assigned Levels of the Research Taxonomy

The conclusions that can be expected from students depend on the level of research that they are performing. Students at the first level, fact-finding, would not be expected to reach any conclusions. At the second level, asking / searching, the students might *find* conclusions, probably short summaries, in their sources. Students will not be likely to find overall conclusions for their research subject at this level of research.

When students are examining / organizing (third level), they will still be working with conclusions offered by others. Although students are examining and reorganizing their evidence at this level, they are concentrating on selection of appropriate information and conclusions rather than on evaluation or original thinking.

By the fourth level of research, evaluating / deliberating, students think about their evidence on a sophisticated level. They investigate all sides of an issue, compare the information, and perhaps draw their own conclusions. Students performing research at this level can be taught the different relationships that can exist among pieces of evidence.

The integrating / concluding or fifth level of research requires students to draw their own conclusions. They internalize the information they find, connect it with their previous knowledge, and develop conclusions based on that evidence. Teaching the types of conclusions outlined earlier in this chapter would help students perform research at this level.

At the sixth level, conceptualizing, students go beyond their conclusion to form an original concept based on the conclusion. If students decide that support for families of alcoholics in their city is poor and unsuccessful (a judgment conclusion), then they design a family-support program that will be more successful.

To help students practice identifying relationships or drawing conclusions in the classroom before a large-scale library research project, teachers can require students to read a specific news magazine article and identify some relationships among information or establish conclusions. Handouts 11.1 and 11.2 can be adapted for this practice. Class discussion or small-group work following this individual preparation will improve students' abilities to see relationships and establish conclusions.

DEVELOP AN OUTLINE FOR THE FINAL PRODUCT

Understanding the Necessity for Outlines

Many teachers remember their own experience with outlining in school; often the process consisted of writing papers first and outlines last. Today's students continue that tradition.

Part of the resistance to outlining may stem from the fact that traditional I-II-III/A-B-C outlines are not appropriate for many writing and research projects. Actually, traditional outlines are more useful to the *reader* than the *writer*. A table of contents is this type of outline (Ellis, 1983). In contrast, an outline to help the *writer* can take another form entirely, ranging from a rough list to an elaborate cluster or diagram.

A number of prewriting organizational methods, both traditional and nontraditional, can be powerful tools for writing. Students can practice the methods described below on classroom assignments before they must use them for complex research projects.

Organizing with a Traditional Outline

The traditional, linear outline can help students organize low-level research projects with simple categories and limited amounts of data. The key words of the research questions serve as the main points on a traditional outline. Because the notes were linked to these main ideas, students can place each supporting idea under the correct main point on the outline.

Problems occur with traditional outlines when students working on high-level research try to sort large amounts of complicated information. The categories are not so easily defined; the relationships between blocks of information may be complex; and creating the outline can be more confusing than helpful.

Visualizing with a Nontraditional Outline

During the 1970s researchers studied the role of the two hemispheres of the brain in learning. At about the same time, some educators began proposing that students add right-brain techniques to their prewriting organizational structures.

Most nontraditional outlining techniques combine the visual and the verbal so that students can *see* the informational relationships within their project. These "outlines" are comparable to creating a clay sculpture; students can move chunks of information easily, trying several organizational patterns. Primary and secondary points become obvious, and merely by changing a few lines, students can create new arrangements which emphasize or de-emphasize specific data.

Visual techniques which allow students to manipulate key ideas include card sets; linear maps; key word cluster maps (also called webbing or mazing); diagrams; and charts. These visualizing methods have been elaborated upon by a number of authors including Philip Hubbard, Linda Verlee Williams, Marilyn Hanf Buckley, Owen Boyle, and Gabriele Lussar Rico.

Card Sets

Arranging and rearranging note cards has been the customary way for students to organize their information. Using *key idea* cards to create an outline, however, is different from using the actual note cards. In fact, the notes should be set aside for the time being. At this point in the process, students should look at patterns rather than at specific data; therefore, they should work only with cards that contain the key words taken from the questions and perhaps with additional cards for important subpoints.

Once the key idea cards have been prepared, students arrange the cards on a flat surface until they discover an arrangement they like. Then they copy the ideas in that order. The card set can be used again if the organization seems awkward at any time during the actual writing.

This technique will not work for all students, but it does have the advantage of a tactile element. Students can physically change the arrangement as many times as they want.

Linear Maps

Students who are comfortable using card sets may also find linear maps useful. While this technique does not encourage quite the same "right brain" involvement as the techniques that follow, it can be a useful bridge between sequential approaches and the more visual techniques which encourage creative information connections. Right-brained Fred at the beginning of this chapter would have responded to visual outlining techniques for his project on diabetes.

DIABETES

Symptoms	*Causes*	*Treatment*
Thirst	Immune system	Weight loss
Frequent urination	Stress	Exercise
Blood sugar	Heredity	Diet
Weakness		Insulin
Nausea		

Key Words/Cluster Maps

Students may have already performed clustering activities earlier in the research process. At this step they cluster their key words and supporting ideas to identify an organizational pattern.

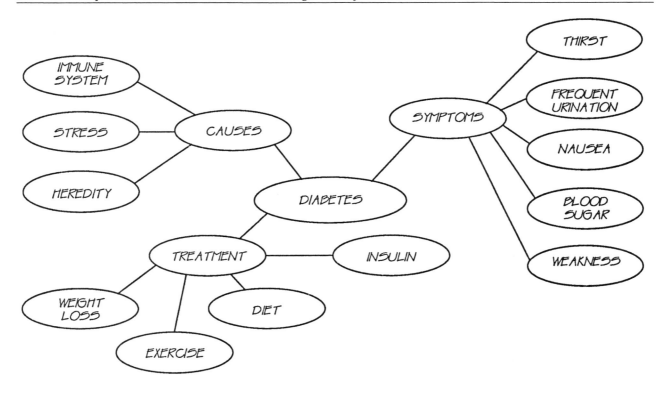

Both linear maps and clusters often lead to an enumerative organization in which the student addresses in turn each subtopic with all its supporting information.

Diagrams

Diagrams are visual arrangements that use pattern and graphic symbols to represent the relationships among ideas. Students will perceive special relationships among data (cause and effect; chronological development) with a diagram visual.

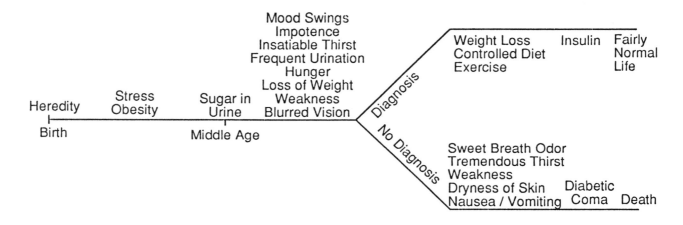

Diabetes Progression

Charts

Charts are especially appropriate for a comparison / contrast approach to a topic. Ideas are listed in columns which can be compared to each other.

Type 1 Diabetes:	*Type 2 Diabetes:*
May be caused by fault in immune system.	May be caused by body's ineffective use of insulin.
No insulin produced by beta cells.	Body cannot use insulin produced by beta cells.
Usually begins before age 30.	Usually begins after age 30.
More serious.	Less serious.
Must be controlled by insulin.	Usually controlled by weight loss, exercise, and diet.
Most people can lead fairly normal lives.	Most people can lead fairly normal lives.

Students find it difficult to write comparison / contrast papers which compare subtopics point by point. Writing about one side and then the other is much simpler. By constructing a chart which sets up a one-to-one comparison on each item, students will see the comparisons and will create an effective comparison / contrast product.

Using the Outline

One would expect students to be able to use their outline and immediately begin work on their final product. Sometimes, however, they need still more thought before writing can begin.

Students can use their outlines to help guide that thought. If the class is working within share groups, members can show their outlines to the others and talk through their products. The group members, who see the plans and hear the explanations, can help refine the organization. Talking through the outline will help establish a fluency of ideas for the final project.

The outlines will also serve as guides for teachers giving individual help and are especially useful in a team-teaching situation. No matter who has previously helped a student, any member of the teaching team can quickly determine the organization of the project from the outline. Students having difficulty with a part of their final project can "talk through" the outline to help identify their errors in organization or logic. A few lines, erasures, or added clusters will probably repair the problem without the pain of rewriting the entire structure.

Because outlines developed in an informal manner will be highly idiosyncratic, teachers should give students a credit grade rather than an evaluative grade for the outline. Insisting that there is only one correct way to organize information blocks creativity. While students must realize that their readers need a logical organization, teachers must realize that several patterns may be logical for the same data.

COMPENSATION FOR THIS STEP

At every research level beyond the lowest (fact-finding), students should think about their research enough to recognize logical conclusions presented by someone else. At the high levels of research, students go beyond understanding others' conclusions to drawing their own. Understanding a conclusion is important to the students' ability to internalize the information, and no one can perform that internalization for the students.

Outlining can be skipped by students only if the research project is highly structured, with every student performing the same research albeit on different topics. If everyone in the class has been assigned to report on a specific mammal, a teacher-prepared outline can be used. Even then, however, students can practice visualizing relationships if the prepared outline is a cluster or mind map. Students can have input if some of the entries or cluster areas are drawn in but left blank for student-located information.

For most research assignments, students must develop their own, personalized outline. The organizational skills they learn will serve them well.

REFLECTION POINT
Are my conclusions based on researched evidence?
Does my outline logically organize conclusions and evidence?

The student should ask:

1. Did I find or draw conclusions supported by research?

2. Do my conclusions support my thesis statement or statement of purpose?

3. Are the various parts of my research arranged in a logical sequence?

IDENTIFYING RELATIONSHIPS

Read the assigned article. Identify and describe an example of each type of relationship that is in the article.

1. PATTERN—Do certain groups described in the article behave in a particular way? Is there any evidence of a cycle—events or attitudes that disappear and reappear?

2. SIMILARITIES AND DIFFERENCES—Can certain people, situations, events, or issues in this article be compared to others about which you know?

3. CAUSE AND EFFECT—Is there an effect which can be directly related to a cause?

    Cause—

    Effect—

4. PART VERSUS WHOLE—Is there a main idea which is supported by two pieces of evidence?

    Main idea—

    Evidence—

    Evidence—

5. CHANGE OVER TIME—Is there a change over time implied in the article?

Handout 11.1. Barbara K. Stripling and Judy M. Pitts, *Brainstorms and Blueprints: Teaching Library Research as a Thinking Process* (Englewood, Colo.: Libraries Unlimited, 1988).

ESTABLISHING CONCLUSIONS

Based on the evidence included in the assigned article, establish each type of conclusion described below.

1. SUMMARY—Write one sentence which expresses the main idea of the article.

2. GENERALIZATION—Write a general statement which you think is true for the events in this article as well as for other similar situations.

3. HYPOTHESIS—Predict what would happen *if some aspect of the subject were changed.*

4. PREDICTION—Based upon the evidence in the article, predict what will happen in the future *if no changes are made in the situation.*

5. SOLUTION—Identify a problem described in the article and suggest a solution.

6. ANALOGY—Compare the situation described in the article to a similar situation with which you are familiar or can research.

7. JUDGMENT—Based upon your own feelings and evidence from the article, make a judgment about a situation described in the article.

Handout 11.2. Barbara K. Stripling and Judy M. Pitts, *Brainstorms and Blueprints: Teaching Library Research as a Thinking Process* (Englewood, Colo.: Libraries Unlimited, 1988).

Chapter 12

STEP TEN
Create and Present Final Product

The mother dove cast a wary eye from a lower branch of the blue spruce tree. Perched precariously alongside was her baby. Suddenly the mother fluttered to a branch about ten feet above. As she scanned the surrounding grass, she kept a watchful eye on her baby.

The baby understood his task—to learn to fly. His mother had obviously taught the basics and modeled the process. But he had just arrived at the safety of this branch; he hesitated to leap into the unknown again. Head bobbing and feathers twitching, he mentally rehearsed the task. Agitated, he tottered back and forth on the branch, head dipping as he stepped.

Finally, stretching his wings and craning his neck, he flew—about eight inches to the next branch. Nine feet more to his goal, the protection of mom. He strutted tentatively on this branch, to test his growing confidence. Again he lifted off—a flight of four feet.

The mother dove took pity. With great patience she fluttered down to her baby, steeling him by her encouraging presence for the great adventure of flying. And fly he did. Tossing his head, he spread his wings and took off. Beyond the extended arms of the tree he sailed. Behind him, ready to assist, perched his mother. As she watched, he settled on the highest branch of an adjacent tree. He could fly.

Teachers and library media specialists, like parent birds, can lay groundwork, give instructions, model behavior, display patience, and supply encouragement. But at the last moment, it is the *students'* task to create and present the final product.

The most successful projects combine information discovered through research with the students' own ideas, opinions, and feelings into a colorful display much as a prism gathers light from various sources and refracts it into a rainbow. Unless students create their own rainbow with the research results, they will have gained only an accumulation of facts which will be quickly forgotten. Their active learning transforms information into knowledge. A Chinese proverb says: "I hear and I forget. I see and I remember. I do and I understand."

The emphasis during most of the research process has been on *critical* thinking skills. During this final step, students will focus on *creative* thinking skills while, at the same time, maintaining a critical attitude toward their researched information.

Creative thinking requires fluency, flexibility, originality, elaboration, and risk taking, all of which can be woven through the process of creating a final product. Students can practice these skills whether they are writing a formal paper, creating a videotape, or composing a letter to a historical person.

The processes of research and creation, because they tap students' critical and creative energies, are actually more important than the final product. Consequently the evaluation of a project should be based on the entire research and creation processes, not solely on the product of those processes. Students who have practiced critical and creative thinking skills during research and production have succeeded in important aspects of the unit. It has been said that we might have to reinvent the wheel every once in awhile, not because we need a lot of wheels, but because we need a lot of inventors.

The classroom teacher and the library media specialist may continue to team teach during this final phase of the research process, or students may return to the classroom. To create a final project, students must be able to:

1. Prewrite or preview the final product.

2. Draft the final product.

3. Revise and edit the final product.

4. Present the final product in an appropriate form.

5. Evaluate their own efforts.

This chapter will not explain the writing process because numerous sources already do so. Instead, it will focus on building creativity into writing about research and on producing visuals based on research.

PREWRITE OR PREVIEW THE FINAL PRODUCT

The whole research process to this point has been prewriting—preparing to write. The students may not have performed every step of the process; however, by the time they reach step ten of the research process, they have thought through their research and have originated or identified conclusions for their evidence. This reasoning has been broadened with creative brainstorming, visualizing, and questioning.

One creative aspect of prewriting is *previewing*—visualizing the final product. Although students will know the format for their final product (as a result of their choice or of the assignment), they probably will not have tried to visualize it. To "see" the final product, students must have internalized their researched information and conclusions.

Immediately prior to the first draft of a project, students find it helpful to reread all their notes (including reactions) at one sitting and to study their outline. If the research project is a major one, teachers should plan some "dead time" into the schedule for unpressured contemplation of the completed research.

DRAFT THE FINAL PRODUCT

The drafting process differs slightly for written and visual products, although both start with a precomposing phase when students review or revise their production timetable (see handout 8.1) and gather necessary materials and equipment.

Drafting a Written Research Paper

Getting Started

Experienced authors find beginning a new writing difficult; the same is true for students. Perhaps students realize that first efforts are often depressingly rough; or perhaps the sheer amount of information associated with a research project overwhelms them. These students will need help in focusing on the goals of their project. They can achieve this concentration by laying out their thesis statement and their visual map or outline whenever they write, giving them constant access to their controlling and supporting ideas, their conclusions, and their organizational plan.

As students begin writing, they should choose surroundings in which they feel comfortable. The place, background activity, and time of day should all contribute to a working atmosphere.

One in-class technique some teachers use to help students get started is to have students freewrite their rough draft during a class period, using their outline but not their notes. Although this situation is traumatic at first, students are often surprised to find that, if they reacted thoughtfully to their notes, they have internalized enough to write their rough draft in this way. With freewriting, students develop fluency and sometimes an original approach that might never have emerged if they had remained fettered to their notes.

Another, more traditional alternative is to have students write rough drafts in class, allowing reference to notes but not to any sources. Students who have difficulty writing those first sentences appreciate teacher encouragement and support during the process. Once the paper is started, most can continue elsewhere.

Expecting first drafts to be rough can help students persist. Improvement is possible only after a project has been committed to paper.

Discovering Creativity

An actor beginning rehearsal for a new production will want to bring originality to the role while maintaining the integrity of the script. Student writers face a similar problem: they must bring some creativity to their final product without allowing that originality to intrude upon the research itself.

Several techniques can help students discover creativity. First, students should view their outline as flexible; strict adherence to an outline can fence out new ideas. Students should rearrange their structure as new relationships occur to them and include new ideas which splinter from old ones. Freewriting and brainstorming can also be used at any point during writing to develop new insights or creative approaches.

Students can be more creative if they allow enough time during the writing for ideas to gel, to take on new forms. Many students think that they can write a research paper in a couple of nights. They may, in fact, be able to sketch out a boring rough draft in that amount of time. But with no time allocated for creative ideas to emerge, students will produce uninspired papers.

Writing aids, such as thesauri or quotation books, can spark creativity. Pictures can also inspire students to write. Photographs of living conditions in the dust bowl can bring America in the 1930s to life.

Overcoming a Writing Block

Students who, despite all efforts, contract the dreaded WRITING BLOCK will need to reuse the techniques described above. They might change their environment or put away their work until a different perspective reveals the problem. A persistent block may indicate a problem with the evidence or arrangement; students may need to think about or talk through their project with a peer or teacher to locate the problem. Writing blocks are not permanent but may require considerable effort to overcome. As Thomas Edison explained: "Genius is one percent inspiration and ninety-nine percent perspiration."

Conforming to a Structure

The techniques listed above will help students write their rough drafts with fluency, flexibility, and originality. Students should also keep in mind the structural aspects to their writing. The main points of their outline should be apparent from the topic sentences and transitional devices within the paper. No extra information should be included. The paper should have a strong introduction and conclusion which reveal or review the focus and supporting points of the paper.

Drafting a Visual Research Project

So many varieties of visual research projects exist that each one cannot be covered in detail. Some principles, however, apply to all. The primary purpose of each visual must be the communication of information that was gathered through the research.

To communicate, a visual must have an *overall theme*, or thesis statement. Students should share it with their audience, either within the visual (through the headline, title, or visual focal point) or as a separate written or oral statement.

Students must prove their thesis idea with evidence distilled to its *major points* and with *supporting details*. For a poster or transparency, the number of supporting ideas must be strictly limited; in a television script, more evidence can be used.

After selection of the ideas to be presented, students should choose a *visual image and layout* to communicate those ideas effectively. On two-dimensional visuals, students can use design techniques to emphasize relationships among ideas. If several equally important ideas support the main thesis, they can be arranged in equal-sized sections or in segments of a circle. A chronological relationship can be expressed with a left-to-right linear or clockwise arrangement, or a comparative, with the two ideas directly opposite each other. A taxonomic pattern can be shown on horizontal levels or on a bull's-eye.

For visuals that are presented as a sequence of events (dramatizations, videotaped programs), relationships of ideas are shown by manipulating time rather than layout. The equal importance of several ideas can be expressed by having a moderator state the thesis, introduce one report, refocus on the theme, then direct the audience's attention to another report. Subjects that take place over a period of time are best treated chronologically. Comparative subjects can be effective if treated by switching back and forth between the ideas.

All visuals should follow the guidelines of being *readable, brief, and simple*. To be readable a visual must be large enough and arranged as the eye moves. Posters and transparencies must be arranged left to right, clockwise, or top to bottom. Readable video productions or live action performances focus audience attention on the action and move at a comfortable pace.

Brief visuals in two dimensions should have no more than ten to twenty words and four to five images per visual. For productions, brief denotes crisp action, no dead time, and no more information than people can absorb at one sitting.

Simple means communicating only one main idea per visual. It also means using white space on two-dimensional visuals and reducing superfluous action in performances.

REVISE AND EDIT THE FINAL PRODUCT

Revising may be the most neglected phase of the writing process. Many (most?) students feel that once a product is created, it is complete. Yet the first product, for any assignment, is only a beginning. The rough edges must be polished through revision or rehearsal until the project can shine proudly before an audience. Whether the revision is completed in the classroom or the library media center, sharing and feedback from peers and/or teachers as well as self-evaluation will be necessary.

Peer/Teacher Sharing and Feedback

Sharing with classmates can be successful on a one-to-one basis or in groups if strict guidelines are in effect. Specific goals, criteria for evaluation, and deadlines are essential. Students can be asked to respond with reader-based feedback (How do the readers respond to the project?) (see handout 12.1) or with criterion-based feedback (How well does the project follow the rules and guidelines of good communication?) (see handout 12.2) (Elbow, 1981).

One-to-one peer sharing can operate in three ways: blind, written comments (using identity codes instead of names); personal, written comments (one student offering written comments to another); or verbal interchanges (two students sharing ideas face-to-face). The teacher monitors carefully the use of the evaluation criteria and the tone of the comments made.

If sharing is done in groups, the composition of each four- to five-member group is determined by the teacher. The essential ingredient for every share group is an emphasis on helping rather than on criticizing. The teacher circulates during share time to ensure that every group is operating in this positive way.

Students may be given practice in critical evaluation skills through whole-class critiquing. The teacher prepares copies of two student research projects from other classes. Students spend the first ten or fifteen minutes of the period reading/viewing a project and filling in the reader-based feedback form (handout 12.1). During a class discussion, students identify the strong points of the project, the areas for improvement, and suggested changes. When the second project is critiqued, the two projects can be compared (Graner, 1987).

Teachers may decide to forego peer sharing, in which case they themselves must evaluate the students' rough drafts. The reader-based or criterion-based feedback forms may be used, or the teacher may offer other comments. Although evaluation of rough drafts is time-consuming, students need the evaluative comments to refocus their thinking before they start to revise.

Self-Evaluating

Students can evaluate their own work by using feedback from teachers or classmates and by asking themselves some questions.

1. Is my main idea clearly communicated?

2. Is my evidence appropriate, accurate, clear, and thorough enough to support the conclusions?

3. Is my evidence presented in the proper order?

4. Are parts of the project not effective? Why?

5. Are my introduction, conclusion, and transitions effective? For visuals, is the layout effective?

Editing

After students have revised their projects, they must turn to editing. At this point they manipulate the language and grammar of the project, rather than the ideas and overall structure.

Editing can be performed by peers or by the students themselves, especially if they are given an editing checklist (see handout 12.3).

Final polishing takes place in this editing phase. Students should seek readers for their papers or projects to help identify every mistake.

PRESENT THE FINAL PRODUCT

Completed projects must be shared. They may be handed in to the teacher, shared with other students in the classroom, put on display in the library media center, or published. The response that students receive from peers is more rewarding than a teacher evaluation. In addition, students learn from each others' research.

If a project is to be shared orally, students must learn presentation skills. The first step in preparing an oral presentation is to *write a clear outline* which includes a unifying idea and four to six supporting ideas. In most cases, this outline will be a simplified version of the one developed at step nine of the research process. To help those listening understand the organization, students can put the outline on a transparency or poster.

Since lectures without visuals or class participation can be boring, students need to *create visuals* for every supporting idea. The visuals may be key words, idea starters, examples, explanations, or whatever else seems appropriate. Students must leave their visuals in place long enough for everyone to absorb the information.

Students preparing an oral presentation should *make the message interesting and clear*. Stories and interesting examples are more important for oral presentations than for written projects. If students use statistics, they can make them understandable with simplified graphs. Complex ideas can be presented in parts and illustrated with clear visuals to help build an understanding. Finally, to make the presentation interesting, students must cut the material and present only the best evidence aloud.

The next stage in preparing an oral presentation is to *work on the delivery.* Four student guidelines are as follows:

1. Work from notes, not from a word-for-word script. Otherwise, the temptation will be to read the script.

2. Keep sentences and words simple; the audience will be listening, not reading.

3. Practice the talk a minimum of three times all the way through, *out loud*, using all props and visuals.

4. Don't rush during the presentation. Use eye contact to involve the audience. Pitch the delivery to someone in the back of the room.

Students can *arouse audience interest* at the beginning of their presentation with an attention-getting quote, statistic, or example. Questions for the audience will encourage active listening. Anything unusual like costumes, props, music, or sound effects will set an interesting mood.

To sustain interest throughout the presentation, students can ask questions periodically, give handouts, or ask class members to participate. Most important for sustaining interest is a lively delivery of thought-provoking information.

To strengthen understanding at the conclusion of oral presentations, students can *encourage class discussion* by waiting for questions or giving a discussion starter.

Teachers who consider assigning oral presentations should weigh the benefits of shared knowledge and presentation experience with the cost of using several class days. For certain projects, alternative display methods might be more effective and less time-consuming. American history students who have researched twentieth-century America might, for example, compile decade books for class browsing or publish a newspaper containing articles on the research. Posters and three-dimensional projects can be displayed around the classroom or in the library media center.

EVALUATE THE FINAL PRODUCT

Student research projects can be evaluated by the teacher, the library media specialist, or the students themselves. The most effective evaluations combine those three.

Although evaluation of research projects should continue throughout the research process, a final evaluation should be performed after the project has been completed. Students or teachers can use an evaluation form that covers both the research process and the final product (see handout 12.4). This form can be easily adapted to reflect any variety of visual or written project requirements.

A simpler alternative for the final evaluation is a Likert form (see handout 12.5). A five-point scale better shows students how they performed on each item than does a "yes/no" judgment.

COMPENSATION FOR THIS STEP

Teachers and library media specialists cannot perform this step of the research process for the students. They can, however, make it easier by working closely with students throughout this final step.

Students will need special help during the revision phase because many have never been expected to revise carefully. Peer revision may provide a variety of insights for students to consider. Word processing facilities will also aid the revision process.

Teachers and library media specialists can best help students with this step of the research process by making sure that students have done well on the preceding steps. Sholem Asch said that "writing comes more easily if you have something to say." Students who have progressed through all the steps of the research process will have something to say.

REFLECTION POINT
Is my paper/project satisfactory?

The student should ask: Is my paper/project the best I can make it?

READER-BASED FEEDBACK

1. What does this project say? Give a one-sentence summary.

2. How did the project make you feel about the subject?

3. Are the main points effectively supported with research? Give examples.

4. What part of the project was most effective? Why?

5. What part of the project was least effective? Why?

6. What could be done to improve weaknesses?

How effective is the presentation of the researched information?

not at all effective			very effective
1	2	3	4

How interesting is this project?

quite dull			very interesting
1	2	3	4

Handout 12.1. (Concept of reader-based feedback adapted from Peter Elbow, *Writing with Power* [New York: Oxford University Press, 1981]). Barbara K. Stripling and Judy M. Pitts, *Brainstorms and Blueprints: Teaching Library Research as a Thinking Process* (Englewood, Colo.: Libraries Unlimited, 1988).

CRITERION-BASED FEEDBACK

Purpose

NI S E 1. Where is this project headed? Does the thesis make this clear?

NI S E 2. Does the project cover only the points included in the thesis, or does it shoot off in new directions?

NI S E 3. Is the writer trying to do too much? Too little?

NI S E 4. Does the author seem to *care* about the project?

Content

NI S E 1. When you're through, can you easily summarize this project?

NI S E 2. Can the reader easily understand it?

NI S E 3. Are there places you found confusing?

NI S E 4. Are there places where the writer said too much or overexplained the subject?

NI S E 5. Do research findings support all the main points?

NI S E 6. Are interesting facts and examples included from the research?

Organization

NI S E 1. Do the main points seem to be in the right order?

NI S E 2. Are the main points linked with logical thought and grammatical connections?

NI S E 3. Does the project begin smoothly? Does it take too long to get started?

NI S E 4. What about the ending? Does it end crisply and excitingly?

NI = Needs Improvement   S = Satisfactory   E = Excellent

Handout 12.2. (Concept of criterion-based feedback adapted from Peter Elbow, *Writing with Power* [New York: Oxford University Press, 1981]). Barbara K. Stripling and Judy M. Pitts, *Brainstorms and Blueprints: Teaching Library Research as a Thinking Process* (Englewood, Colo.: Libraries Unlimited, 1988).

EDITING CHECKLIST

Work through the project several times looking for the errors or weaknesses described below. Concentrate on usage the first time through, on mechanics the second time, and on proper credit for ideas the third time.

I. Usage

Subject/verb disagreement
Wrong tense/verb form
Passive verbs
Wrong word choice
Necessary word omitted/extra words included

II. Mechanics

Punctuation
Missing, misplaced or unnecessary apostrophes
Missing or unnecessary quotation marks
Missing or unnecessary commas
Missing punctuation at end of sentence

Spelling
Missing or unnecessary capitals
Misspelled words

Sentences
Run-on sentences
Fragments
Lack of parallel structure in series
Lack of varied sentence structure

Paragraphs
Unrelated information within paragraph
Too long or too short for readability

III. Footnotes and Bibliography

No credit given for ideas and quotations
Incorrect format

Handout 12.3. Barbara K. Stripling and Judy M. Pitts, *Brainstorms and Blueprints: Teaching Library Research as a Thinking Process* (Englewood, Colo.: Libraries Unlimited, 1988).

RESEARCH PROJECT FINAL EVALUATION FORM

THE RESEARCH PROCESS

Y N   1.   Does the project adequately cover material available on the topic?

Y N   2.   Is the thesis of the project clear?

Y N   3.   Does the project fully develop all the ideas in the thesis?

Y N   4.   Are all the main ideas supported with researched facts and examples?

Y N   5.   Do the conclusions follow from the main ideas and supporting information?

Y N   6.   Does the project follow a logical organization?

Y N   7.   Are all facts that are not "common knowledge" footnoted?

THE WRITING PROCESS

Y N   1.   Are the grammar and mechanics correct?

Y N   2.   Are verb tenses consistent?

Y N   3.   Is sentence structure varied?

Y N   4.   Does each paragraph have a topic sentence?

Y N   5.   Does each paragraph relate to the main topic?

Y N   6.   Do transitional words and devices smooth the flow of ideas?

Y N   7.   Does the project include a clear introduction and conclusion?

THE PHYSICAL REQUIREMENTS

Y N   1.   Has the project been produced as required?

Y N   2.   Is the project neat and pleasing in appearance?

Y N   3.   Are footnotes and bibliography included as required?

Handout 12.4. Barbara K. Stripling and Judy M. Pitts, *Brainstorms and Blueprints: Teaching Library Research as a Thinking Process* (Englewood, Colo.: Libraries Unlimited, 1988).

RESEARCH PAPER EVALUATION

THESIS

Your project does not carry out the ideas in your thesis statement.

Your project reflects only part of the ideas included in your thesis.

You have managed a perfect match between your thesis and your project.

1   2   3   4   5

STRUCTURE

I get lost among your main points; the arrangement is not logical.

Your project would be clearer if you rearranged the main ideas and added more transitional phrases.

The main points fit together logically and the structure is easy to follow.

1   2   3   4   5

RESEARCHED EVIDENCE

You have not included enough researched evidence—facts, examples, statistics—for your main points.

Some of your main points are supported with research, but others are not.

Great job! You have used research to support every main idea.

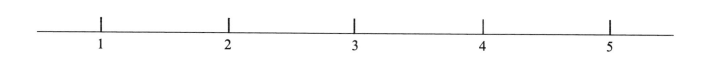

1   2   3   4   5

(Research Paper Evaluation continues on page 148.)

FORMAT

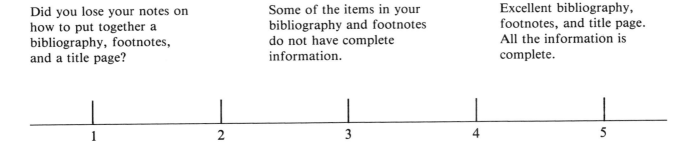

Did you lose your notes on how to put together a bibliography, footnotes, and a title page?

Some of the items in your bibliography and footnotes do not have complete information.

Excellent bibliography, footnotes, and title page. All the information is complete.

```
1        2        3        4        5
```

MECHANICS, SPELLING, PUNCTUATION

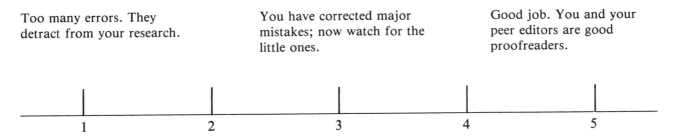

Too many errors. They detract from your research.

You have corrected major mistakes; now watch for the little ones.

Good job. You and your peer editors are good proofreaders.

```
1        2        3        4        5
```

OVERALL IMPRESSION

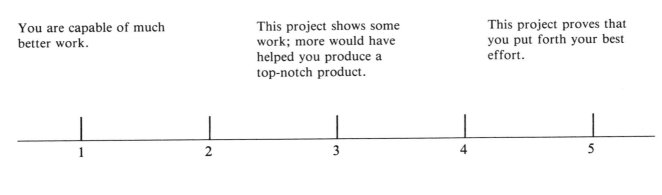

You are capable of much better work.

This project shows some work; more would have helped you produce a top-notch product.

This project proves that you put forth your best effort.

```
1        2        3        4        5
```

Grand Average Rating: _____

Handout 12.5. Barbara K. Stripling and Judy M. Pitts, *Brainstorms and Blueprints: Teaching Library Research as a Thinking Process* (Englewood, Colo.: Libraries Unlimited, 1988).

Chapter 13

RESEARCH AS A THINKING PROCESS
Preparing Students in the Classroom

By the time Mr. Carlson had finished presenting "Browsing in the *Readers' Guide*" to the class of twenty-nine seventh graders, he knew their popcorn juices were on the verge of exploding.

"You have the rest of the period today to find a book or magazine on your subject and start taking notes."

As one giant kernel, the students popped up to pursue their research topics. Mr. Carlson smiled as he thought about how well these students had been prepared by their teacher in the classroom for this library research assignment. Mrs. Duncan had done everything he had asked and more. The students had come in with their topics, anxious to seek out new ideas. They had been using learning logs all year, so notetaking would be easy for them.

"Mrs. Duncan, I think we've done it. These kids seem to be *thinking* about their research." Mr. Carlson couldn't suppress a self-satisfied grin as he started a tour through the library to see who needed help.

When he turned the corner, he spotted Curtis wandering along the magazine storage shelves, talking softly to himself. Anxious to be of help, Mr. Carlson stepped forward just enough to overhear Curtis singing softly, "A, B, C, D...E, F, G...."

"Oh, well," Mr. Carlson sighed, "twenty-eight out of twenty-nine isn't too bad." Later, as he described the scene to Mrs. Duncan, they laughed at themselves for expecting every student to be ready for high-level research skills.

Actual preparation for library research begins in the classroom well before a particular assignment is designed. Teachers can establish an atmosphere that positively affects students' attitudes toward learning and researching. Teachers can also help students develop skills in questioning, thinking, writing, planning, producing, and revising, all of which will transfer to library research. Finally, research preparation activities conducted in the classroom can address particular trouble spots in research (like notetaking or paraphrasing).

ATMOSPHERE IN THE CLASSROOM

Learning takes place in classrooms where teachers and students actively seek new ideas. This atmosphere of inquiry is fostered by the teacher; it solidifies when students recognize that learning is continuous, that it involves certain skills, and that knowing how to learn is more valuable than knowing specific bits of information.

Teachers can introduce the spirit of inquiry by providing information beyond the textbook through lectures, guest speakers, current newspaper and magazine articles, handouts, and audiovisual presentations. Students should be held responsible for learning and sometimes for supplying additional information.

Teachers can also use questioning techniques to stimulate active learning and draw students into an interchange of ideas. The techniques include using open-ended, high-level questions (such as "why?" or "how?" or "what if?"); waiting at least three seconds after a question before calling on a student; responding to students in a thoughtful way; restating students' answers and asking for amplification or clarification; and giving credibility to students' answers by writing them for other students to see.

Making the classroom a center for exchanging ideas has several positive implications for library research: students come to the library on their own to seek information to present in class; students develop an openness to new ideas; and students become interested in a range of topics that were previously unknown to them. When it is time to pick a research topic, these students may no longer groan, "I'm not interested in anything."

In addition to a spirit of inquiry in the classroom, an attitude of group cooperation will lead to better library research. Because many research activities culminate with group presentations, teachers can use group projects in the classroom to develop human relations, co-planning, and cooperation skills.

Teachers should always set clear guidelines for group work. The members should choose a presentation format, construct an outline, and divide responsibility. Individuals should be able to prove their contributions to the group effort by turning in notes and a bibliography and by participating directly in the presentation.

SKILLS IN THE CLASSROOM

During a library research project, many specific research skills will be taught by the teacher or library media specialist. Students will be more successful at library research, however, if they have already practiced specific learning skills in their classroom work. These skills, which include questioning, thinking, writing, planning, producing, and revising, can be incorporated into curricular units for any subject area.

Questioning

Assigning the questioning role to students can elevate the level of student thinking, but teachers will have to help students with their questioning skills. Following the reading of a textbook chapter or the viewing of an audiovisual program, students can be assigned to write several pertinent questions which they would like to have answered by their classmates. The questions should range from simple review to ones that will elicit thoughtful discussion. Because these questions may involve speculation, the questioners need not know the answers, but they need to care about discussing the issue.

Based on the learning objectives, teachers select questions to be used in class. By consciously choosing questions from everyone over a period of time, teachers can involve all students in the class interaction (Schaffer, 1987).

Thinking

Many activities in the classroom encourage the development of creative and critical thinking skills, both essential for performing thoughtful library research. Two creative activities—brainstorming and clustering—can be used anytime to help students see new ideas and relationships. If a science student has brought in information about an infant heart transplant, the teacher may ask students to brainstorm about ethical issues that affect the medical field. The resulting cluster includes topics for further class discussion or research and gives students simultaneous experience in brainstorming and clustering.

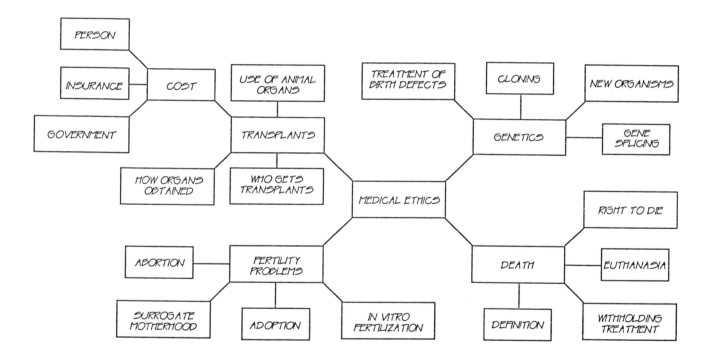

Students also need practice in critical thinking. Taking notes from lectures, audiovisual programs, or written materials can provide experience in recognizing main ideas and supporting details. Some teachers develop notetaking outlines to help students identify important information. As the school year progresses, the teacher-prepared outlines contain fewer specifics, thus requiring more student thought.

Class reading assignments can give students practice in forming opinions and supporting them with specific, well-thought-out reasons. If students do not like a poem they have been assigned to evaluate, they must justify their dislike. Is the vocabulary too difficult? Does the poet seem pretentious? Are the ideas too practical for the poetic format? The students' opinions are less important than the reasoned support they offer.

Another thinking skill important for library research is recognizing relationships among items of information. In other words, students should find similarities and differences, recognize causes and effects, and differentiate generalizations from specific details. Thoughtful teacher questioning can lead students to these distinctions. In addition, handouts 11.1 and 11.2 can provide practice in identifying relationships or establishing conclusions with any curricular materials.

Writing

Writing can be a catalyst for thinking. H. L. Mencken said, "There is in writing the constant joy of sudden discovery, of happy accident." Unfortunately, many students seldom experience this "joy of sudden discovery" because they are rarely asked to write.

Thinking-through-writing can be incorporated into any subject area through the use of learning logs, which were described as an effective notetaking technique in chapter 10. Any subject-area notes (even mathematics problems and science experiments) can be taken in the left column. On the right, students may express an opinion, write a question, relate the information to previous knowledge, or summarize. After students have used learning logs for several weeks, the thought level in class discussion and written assignments increases significantly.

Freewriting and directed freewriting (as described in chapter 4) will also generate student thinking. Short directed freewriting activities such as "entry" and "exit" tickets will help students focus on issues. On the tickets (often 3-by-5-inch cards), students respond to a thought question presented by the teacher. Their individual responses serve as a basis for class discussion.

Essays and essay test questions also allow students to display their thoughts on paper. Teachers will find it helpful to review the formation of a thesis statement and a rough outline before students begin writing.

Planning

Because many students lack planning skills, teachers making long-term assignments often provide a step-by-step process and interim deadlines. Teachers can help students acquire their own planning skills by progressing from setting up the entire process, to having class members set activities and interim deadlines, to requiring students to develop individual plans responsive to their own learning styles and schedules.

Producing

Students enjoy producing oral or visual reactions to information and almost any unit can include production of posters, transparencies, videotapes, panel discussions, debates, or individual oral presentations. The library media specialist can teach production skills as needed for each assignment. If students use these alternative presentation formats on several assignments, they build a repertoire of skills for later research presentations.

Revising

As much as possible, students should be held responsible for their own revising and editing. Ideally, teachers should not receive projects which still contain questionable reasoning, awkward wording, poor visual composition, or grammatical or punctuation errors. The revising and editing processes can be handled with various types of peer revision, with teacher feedback, or with self-evaluation. Teachers should provide guidance through checklists and evaluation forms.

RESEARCH PREPARATION ACTIVITIES

Because research projects require many skills, students will benefit from carefully structured, in-class practice before beginning individual work.

If the final product is to be written, students should practice the required expository structure before beginning the research project. Students might write in class a three-point paragraph containing a topic sentence and three supporting details. Later this structure can be transferred to a library research project.

Group research activities can give individual practice in notetaking, organizing information, drawing conclusions, and writing. If students are studying a specific topic, like the California gold rush, each student can be assigned to locate ten facts in library sources. Students share aloud one fact each, and everyone takes notes on the information. As a class or as individuals, students organize the information, write a thesis, and then complete an essay on the topic.

Another research preparation activity includes specific work on paraphrasing and footnoting. The teacher and the library media specialist can make available to the students four or five sources with information on a specific topic. Students use those sources for a practice research paper. This activity allows students to work through many of the research process steps within the confines of limited materials.

In-class practice can lessen anxiety about research. When students begin individual library research projects, they will be familiar with research and writing skills and will be able to concentrate on complex thinking skills.

Students who are building toward major research projects should be working with a teacher who has established a positive atmosphere in the classroom and who has worked on creative and critical thinking skills—the brainstorms and blueprints necessary for performing research as a thinking process. Students need guided practice if they are to replace memorizing and copying with thoughtful learning characterized by questioning, thinking, writing, planning, producing, and revising. Once the atmosphere and some of the skills have been practiced, a successful research unit can begin.

Chapter 14

RESEARCH AS A
THINKING PROCESS
Weaving the Program into the Curriculum

This book has presented a program for planning and teaching library research as a thinking process in any secondary curricular area. Research projects require a substantial investment of time and energy. Why, then, do so many teachers and library media specialists espouse the integration of research into the curriculum? The answer is simple: They have seen the explosions of excitement within students when research subjects become personal and important in their lives. Students reach new levels of thought as they seek, find, analyze, evaluate, assimilate, and communicate new information. The skills they master are lifelong learning skills that will increase their effectiveness as citizens, consumers, and employees.

For students to gain these skills most successfully, the research program must be tightly bound to a school's curriculum. Library media specialists must have as their goal the weaving of a "research strand" into every area of the curriculum. This integration must begin with the adoption of a schoolwide research philosophy and goals. The more that faculty members are involved in the planning and implementation of the philosophy and goals for research, the more they will feel ownership for the concepts included and will enthusiastically support research projects.

The process for weaving a research program into the curriculum is outlined below and discussed in the following pages. The first two steps, laying the foundation and achieving support, will be performed only once in each school when the program is first being set up; the yearly implementation of the program will build on these steps.

Person or Group	*Activity*
Laying the Foundation	
LMS with advisory committee	Develop preliminary ideas for philosophy and goals of research.
LMS with advisory committee	Prepare philosophy and goals.
Achieving Support	
District Curriculum Committee and/or Building Curriculum Committee and/or Building Faculty	Accept philosophy and goals of research.
LMS	Develops skills continuum based on research philosophy and goals.
LMS and department heads or faculty advisory committee	Make tentative assignment of skills to appropriate departments.
LMS	Presents simplified list or matrix of skills to faculty.
LMS	May present workshop about research to faculty.
LMS and faculty and/or departments	Finalize skills assignments.
Implementing the Program	
With departments	
LMS and departments	Insert skills into specific units.
With individual teachers	
LMS and individual teachers	Plan and schedule unit activities.
With administrators	
LMS	Communicates information about the research program.
Evaluating the Program	
LMS	Evaluates class performance, quantity and quality of research units.
LMS and teachers	Change research units to respond to evaluation results.

LAYING THE FOUNDATION

The foundation of a successful research program that extends throughout the curriculum is a philosophy statement and listing of goals for research. These should amplify sections of a library media center philosophy and goals which are already in place, but they should be separated from the more general library media center document so that all teachers can recognize that research goals are their goals, not just the library media center's goals.

Library media specialists can effectively develop preliminary plans for the research philosophy and goals by working with an advisory committee of teachers, administrators, parents, students, and recent graduates. The group, brainstorming in a round-robin fashion, offers completing phrases for a statement such as, "I believe that students performing research should ..." or "I believe that research should...." All ideas should be recorded; no judgment of quality should be made during the brainstorming session.

Library media specialists then categorize the brainstormed phrases as appropriate for either the philosophy or the goals, smooth the language, eliminate duplication, and make the ideas parallel. Working from those ideas, the library media specialist prepares a working draft of the philosophy and goals and then presents it to the advisory committee for revision (see appendix 1 for a sample).

ACHIEVING SUPPORT

In order for a research strand to be integrated into a curriculum, the district and school must provide support. Library media specialists should ask for acceptance of the philosophy and goals by the appropriate district and building curriculum committees, as well as by the building faculty. Each group should be given an opportunity to preview the documents and to offer suggestions for changes.

While the philosophy and goals will provide the foundation for integrating library research into every area of the curriculum, the program will gain widespread faculty support only after specific objectives or skills have been established, preferably on a continuum. The continuum should be developed by the library media specialist with an awareness of the grades at which new levels of the research taxonomy are introduced (see chart in chapter 1) and an understanding of the thinking skills necessary for each step of the research process.

A sample research skills continuum included in appendix 2 is for grades seven through twelve and is based on the assumption that the first levels of research, and the skills necessary for performing those levels, have been taught in grades three through six. Several states and school districts have also published continuums for library media programs from which research skills may be extracted.

Once the research skills continuum has been developed, library media specialists (ideally working with department heads or a faculty advisory committee) can make tentative "assignments" of particular skills to specific subject areas.

Because a skills continuum is often a lengthy, detailed document, library media specialists should consider developing a chart or matrix to display summarized skill responsibilities for all curricular areas of the school (see sample matrix in appendix 3). Alternately, a matrix can be developed for each department to show the specific skills assigned to that one department (see sample matrix in appendix 4).

The matrix (or matrices), which shows skills assignments, can be presented to the faculty for final approval. Depending upon the background of the faculty members, library media specialists may want to offer a rationale for a schoolwide research program and suggest the implications of such a program for the teachers. For example, teachers will be responsible for evaluating the library collection in their subject area, for recommending new materials to be purchased, and for participating in team planning and teaching with the library media specialist. The presentation might also include concrete planning ideas (such as the research and reactions taxonomies and the research process) which will help teachers visualize how the program will fit into their existing curriculum.

IMPLEMENTING THE PROGRAM

Working with Departments

After the entire faculty has accepted the research skills assignments, library media specialists are ready to meet with departments to insert skills into specific units which are already a part of the curriculum or plan new units which will incorporate the research skills.

If seventh-grade science classes study human diseases, a research project could be required which would include appropriate research skills.

Science, Grade 7

Obtaining overview of subject and identifying central issues in it.

Writing statement of purpose.

Writing factual research questions for the appropriate level of research.

Thinking of narrower, broader, and related subject headings.

Using periodical index.

Locating essential information in a variety of types of sources using the table of contents and index.

Taking appropriate notes that answer research questions and avoid plagiarism.

Drafting the final product.

Seventh-grade social studies classes might debate current issues, and thus could be assigned some analysis and database skills.

Social Studies, Grade 7

Recognizing databases as sources of information and as tools for organizing information using standardized categories.

Using a variety of sources.

Assessing accuracy of information.

Determining importance of evidence.

Compiling a bibliography.

Categorizing information.

Developing an outline from a model.

Presenting the final product.

Assigning skills to specific subject areas and grade levels does not eliminate those skills from other subjects and grades; it simply ensures that every research skill will be included somewhere and that no research assignment will overwhelm students with new skills.

Working with Individual Teachers

Once the research skills have been placed on a continuum, a research strand has been inserted into the curriculum, and research skills have been assigned to subjects or units, the library media specialist can plan and schedule unit activities with individual teachers. In some cases, if no real curricular structure exists within a school, individual faculty members will be the only avenue for placing research units within appropriate classes.

Working with the variety of personalities represented on any faculty can be challenging. Some teachers will want to plan and teach every detail of the unit themselves despite the library media specialist's expertise; others will depend on the library media specialist to develop and control the unit. Library media specialists must set a teamwork atmosphere in which each member contributes equally to the unit.

Once research units have been developed, they can be scheduled by the library media specialist and teachers. Keeping in mind the continuum of skills, the school's curriculum, the library's schedule, and individual teacher preferences, the library media specialist can try to distribute research projects throughout the year.

Besides working with teachers to schedule library research units in a variety of curricular areas, the library media specialist must also work to boost the thought level of the research units. If a science teacher, for example, routinely requires students to research current scientific topics, source evaluation skills might be integrated into the activity. As new research units or new teachers are added, the library media specialist can help teachers *consciously* choose high-level assignments. Without this conscious decision, thought levels will drift down to fact-finding, which is usually lower than the students' capabilities and the teachers' intent.

To encourage research-unit renewal, library media specialists can share research-project ideas gathered from professional journals and conferences. Sometimes these ideas will appeal to a particular teacher and form the basis for an exciting research unit.

In any event, the library media specialist should make the collection responsive to the research needs of each teacher's curriculum. If a class discovers that materials on a particular topic are inadequate, the library media specialist should purchase new items on that subject before the next year. Notices of all materials added for specific units should be sent to individual teachers.

Working with Administrators

District and building administrators should be well aware of the library media center's major goals. These goals, which should be presented to the administrators yearly, must include the development of critical thinking skills through research. When the research-across-the-curriculum program is first being developed, the administrators' voice will determine the faculty acceptance of the program and the ease with which it is integrated throughout the curriculum of the school.

Once the program is in place, the library media specialist can encourage continued administrative support by informing the administrators regularly about library media center activities. At the end of the year, an evaluation of the library media center program can review the specific units which helped students develop critical thinking and research skills.

Administrators should regularly be invited to visit the library media center during research units. They may observe the library media specialist teaching part of a unit or watch the teacher and library media specialist working with individual students. Drop-in visits by administrators should be encouraged.

Many schools hold regular meetings of administrators and department heads to discuss curricular matters; library media specialists should be included in these gatherings. When appropriate, the library media specialist should advocate the use of research activities to reach specific curricular objectives. In addition, by participating in curricular planning, the library media specialist will be able to anticipate future research demands on the collection.

EVALUATING THE PROGRAM

Building a program that integrates library research throughout the curriculum of the school is an ongoing process. To ensure that the needs of students, teachers, and library media specialists are being met, every research program should include an evaluation component. The library media specialist can evaluate three aspects to determine the effectiveness of the research-as-a-thinking-process program: class performance, quantity of research units, and quality of research units.

Class Performance

Class performance is assessed to determine the effectiveness of the assignment and the library skills instruction. Although a controlled study could be used to evaluate different approaches to research, most library media specialists have neither the time nor the inclination for such efforts. Fortunately, useful information can be gathered through simpler methods.

One method of evaluating class performance is to assess student products in terms of the sources used and the quality of the research. The library media specialist can analyze the citations and bibliographies of a random sampling of the completed projects by tallying the types, levels, and copyright dates of sources and the number of citations to each.

To evaluate the content, the library media specialist can analyze the projects for level of research indicated by the thesis statement, quality of evidence cited, and quality of conclusions (see appendix 5 for a sample evaluation form for tallying class performance).

A second method to assess the class performance is to evaluate in-progress items (notes, learning logs, rough drafts) after the paper has been turned in and graded. By analyzing the component parts of the research projects, the library media specialist may be able to determine which areas of the instruction were most effective and which were least effective. If many notes seem to be plagiarized or unnecessary, then improvement is needed in the teaching of notetaking skills. If the notes do not answer the research questions, then the library skills instruction should emphasize connection between information needs and notes taken.

The class performance may also be evaluated by interviewing a random sample of students about their perceptions of their own research. The following questions may be used:

1. How did you decide on your topic?

2. How did you know what information to look for?

3. How did you find your best sources?

4. What libraries did you use?

5. Did you find all the information you wanted or needed to find?

6. What aspect of the instruction helped you the most?

7. What would have helped you do a better job?

Evaluation of class performance is an ongoing process which should be conducted often during the year.

Quantity of Research Units

At the end of each month, semester, or year, the library media specialist can count the number of research units completed since the last count. It would be helpful to tally the number of units, the number of *different* teachers, and the number of departments involved, as well as the number of hours of instruction by the library media specialist. In addition, the number of research units which could not be accommodated should be tallied.

The results obtained will not magically rate the success or failure of the research program, but they can be used by the library media specialist in making certain judgments. First, the numbers can be collected to allow comparison with other months, semesters, or years. Seasonal variations can be expected, but a gradual increase should be expected for several years after the research program is first integrated into the curriculum. The number of units will, of course, level off at some point, depending on the capacity of the library media program.

The numbers can be used as justification for increased budget funds, special grant monies, additional aide time, additional professional time—whatever would help the library media program fulfill the demand for research materials, facilities, and instruction.

The data collected can also be used to set goals for the following year. If most of the research units were through the English department, and social studies classes were rarely scheduled, the library media specialist could target the social studies curriculum for research projects in the coming year.

Quality of Research Units

Assessing the quality and level of the research units performed will be subjective. If the library media specialist has used the unit planning sheet recommended in chapter 3 (see handout 3.1), then the level of research and reactions has already been decided. Otherwise the library media specialist will have to make that judgment at this time.

After tallying the research levels of the units, the library media specialist can determine the average level of research performed in the library. A baseline for one year can be established, and then the library media specialist can try to boost some of the fact-finding units to higher levels the next year. No library media specialist should be dismayed that fact-finding research is being performed; at times, that is the most appropriate level for a particular assignment.

While assessing the quality of the research units, the library media specialist might also evaluate the level of skills included in the library instruction. For a library-research-as-a-thinking-process program to be in place, the library media specialist must be instructing students in more than locational skills. Some analysis and evaluation skills must be included for high-level assignments. Underlying all the instruction should be a solid research process.

The Effect of Evaluation

Looking critically at the past enables a library media specialist to strengthen the research program for the future. A continuous process of evaluation leads to an evolving program that corrects failures, builds on successes, and meets the changing needs of students and teachers.

CONCLUSION

The strategies and activities presented throughout this book for working with students and faculty members are not necessarily the "right" solutions to the problem of unthinking research. They do offer alternatives to help library media specialists and teachers boost the level of thought in student research. Perhaps the suggestions offered in this book should be labeled "idea starters," because teachers and library media specialists should adopt and adapt as their own situations warrant.

The underlying key to successful research remains constant no matter what strategies are used: The *process* of thoughtful research is more important than the *product*; the process of research must become the framework for building successful library units *in all areas of the curriculum*. Together, teachers and library media specialists can create assignments and teach skills that will lead students through a thoughtful research process.

Ultimately, the students themselves determine the success of a research-as-a-thinking-process program. Teachers and library media specialists cannot think about research for the students; the students must experience it for themselves. And once they do, then Jason, Julie, Sarah, Patty, Steven, Susan, Matt, Stephanie, Geoffrey, Jennifer and Fred will never go back to copying, "The brown bear is brown."

APPENDIX 1—LIBRARY RESEARCH

Philosophy

The purpose of library research is for students to find, select, evaluate, and use information to enhance their understanding of a subject.

Goals

1. Students will perform library research in every appropriate curricular area.

2. Students will follow a research process to provide structure for their research.

3. Students will develop critical thinking skills by performing thoughtful research.

4. Students will work up through a taxonomy of thoughtful research after they achieve success at each level.

5. Students will be required to react to every research assignment by creating a product or using the information in some way.

APPENDIX 2—RESEARCH SKILLS CONTINUUM

(The skills listed are those *introduced* at each level.)

	Grade 7	Grade 8	Grade 9
Research Process	Level of Research: Evaluating/Deliberating	Level of Research: Evaluating/Deliberating	Level of Research: Evaluating/Deliberating
Choose a Broad Topic	Recognizing researchable topics	Choosing a topic from materials available	
Get an Overview of the Topic	Obtaining an overview from a general encyclopedia Identifying central issues		Recognizing alternate overview sources such as subject encyclopedias and magazine articles
Narrow the Topic	Narrowing topics chronologically, geographically, topically	Relating topic choice to length of project	Narrowing topics to a problem or question
Develop Thesis or Statement of Purpose	Writing a statement of purpose		Writing a thesis statement which can be supported with research
Formulate Questions to Guide Research	Writing factual research questions for the appropriate level of research		
Plan for Research and Production	Following a research and production plan laid out by the teacher	Designing a simple search strategy Planning a presentation	Being aware of a step-by-step research process
Find/ Analyze/ Evaluate Sources	Thinking of narrower, broader, and related subject headings Locating essential information in a variety of types of sources using table of contents and index Using cross references Using word-by-word alphabetization in card catalog Using periodical index Recognizing databases as sources of information and as tools for organizing information using standard categories Using community resources and libraries Using a variety of sources	Using reference materials related to a specific subject or course (subject encyclopedias, dictionaries, atlases) Retrieving information (offline) from a commercial database program Using biographical reference materials Using a simple search strategy	Locating essential information using skimming, scanning, and contextual clues Analyzing sources in terms of appropriateness, usefulness, and currency Evaluating each source in terms of its intended audience

Grade 10	Grade 11	Grade 12
Level of Research: Integrating/Concluding	Level of Research: Integrating/Concluding	Level of Research: Conceptualizing

Choosing a researchable
  topic based on personal interest
  or subject area
		Choosing a topic that can
		  lead to original concepts

	Reading widely to obtain an overview	
Relating topic choice to thought level of research		
Writing a thesis to lead to interpretive research		
Writing interpretive questions leading to conclusions		

Designing a thoughtful
  search strategy
	Choosing the most appropriate
	  presentation format
	Developing a research and
	  production plan
		Targeting an audience beyond
		  school

Using a thoughtful search
  strategy (plan, search, find,
  analyze, evaluate)
Building a list of subject headings
  by using tracings, subject
  heading sources, and
  database thesauri
Using process of browsing
  in regular collection and
  magazine indexes
Using the reference collection
Observing online database
  searching
Using primary sources
Recognizing procedure for
  interlibrary loan
	Using specialized reference
	  materials
	Selecting an appropriate
	  database and planning,
	  executing, and evaluating an
	  online search
	Using bibliographies to find
	  additional information
	Analyzing sources in terms of
	  scope, arrangement, depth of
	  treatment, special features
	Evaluating reliability of
	  each source
		Using advanced search
		  strategies
		Using advanced indexes,
		  thesauri, and online searching
		Using specialized libraries
		  or library collections

(Appendix 2—Research Skills Continuum
continues on page 164.)

Appendix 2—Research Skills Continuum—*Continued*

	Grade 7	Grade 8	Grade 9
Evaluate Evidence/ Take Notes/ Compile Bibliography	Assessing accuracy of information Determining importance of evidence Taking appropriate notes that answer research questions and avoid plagiarism Documenting direct quotations from source materials Compiling a bibliography	Using citation, summary, paraphrase, or quotation notes as appropriate Differentiating among facts, opinions, and values	Understanding importance of using multiple references and comparing them Determining point of view Distinguishing bias from reason Recognizing all sides to an issue Identifying information that should be documented in the final product
Establish Conclusions/ Organize Information into an Outline	Categorizing information Identifying possible conclusions Developing an outline from a model Organizing information with a commercial database program	Developing an original outline to guide creation of the final product	Supporting thesis statement with evidence Recognizing conclusions that are best supported by the evidence
Create and Present Final Product	Drafting, revising, and editing the final product Presenting the final product	Using a variety of audiovisual production skills Using oral presentation skills	Using peer revision and editing

Grade 10	Grade 11	Grade 12
Distinguishing relevant from irrelevant information Taking careful notes and reacting to them with questions, reasons, emotions	Evaluating information within sources Evaluating completeness of research	Recognizing fallacies of reasoning
Identifying relationships among data Integrating information with what is already known Following a process for drawing own conclusion: summary, generalization, solution	Following a process for drawing own conclusion: hypothesis, prediction, analogy, judgment Using a variety of techniques to create an outline	Creating a new concept based on research
Using standard bibliographic and documentation formats	Using self-evaluation for revising and editing	Presenting final product to extended audience through publication or oral presentation

APPENDIX 3—RESEARCH SKILLS ACROSS THE CURRICULUM

	GRADE 10	GRADE 11	GRADE 12

ENGLISH	Research process
	Search strategy
	Notetaking
	Conclusions
		Specialized reference materials
		Online database search
		Analysis of sources
		Evaluation of sources
			Advanced search
			  strategies
			Evaluation of
			  sources & evidence

SOCIAL STUDIES	Research process
	Search strategy
	Subject headings
	Reference collection
	Primary sources
	Conclusions
		Extended reading for overview
		Use of bibliographies
		Analysis of sources
		Evaluation of evidence
			Advanced search
			  strategies
			Creation of new
			  concept based
			  on research

SCIENCE	Research process
	Interpretive
	  research
	  questions
	Online database
	  search
	  observation
	Interlibrary loan
		Specialized reference materials
		Evaluation of sources
		Evaluation of evidence
		Online database search
			Advanced indexes
			  and thesauri

MATH	Reference collection	Specialized reference materials	Research skills as needed

FINE ARTS	Browsing processes	Evaluation of completeness
		  of research
			Research skills as
			  needed

BUSINESS/ VOCATIONAL	Interlibrary loan	Online database search	Research skills as needed

HEALTH/P.E.	Subject headings
	Online database
	  search
	  observation
	Interlibrary loan
		Online database search
		Evaluation of completeness
		  of research
			Research skills as
			  needed

FOREIGN LANGUAGE	Reference collection	Choice of presentation format	Research skills as needed

APPENDIX 4 — LIBRARY SKILLS FOR ENGLISH RESEARCH ASSIGNMENTS

(The skills listed are those *introduced* at each level.)

	Grade 10		Grade 11		Grade 12	
B A S I C	Research process Database search observation Browsing processes Subject headings Production Notetaking	Research Project	Use of reference collection Choice of presentation format	Research Essay	Analysis of sources	Essays
R E G U L A R	Research process Database search observation Browsing processes Subject headings Production Use of reference collection Notetaking Support for thesis Conclusions	Research Project	Analysis of sources Introduction to other libraries and classification systems Database use Specialized reference materials Evaluation of sources	Research Essay Research Paper	Evaluation of information within a source Creation of new concept	Essays
A C C E L E R A T E D	Research process Database search observation Search strategy Browsing processes Subject headings Production Use of reference collection Analysis of sources Notetaking Support for thesis Conclusions	Research Essay	Evaluation of sources Evaluation of information within a source Database use Introduction to other libraries and classification systems Use of bibliographies Evaluation of completeness of research	Research Essay Research Paper	Creation of new concept Advanced search strategies Advanced indexes and thesauri	Essays

APPENDIX 5—TALLY FORM FOR CLASS PERFORMANCE
ON LIBRARY RESEARCH

Description of Assignment:

Source Evaluation:

Sources	# Used	# Citations
Magazines Popular		
Informational		
Scholarly		
Secondary sources		
Primary sources		
General encyclopedias		
Specialized reference books		
Government documents		
Vertical file materials		
Audiovisuals		

Copyright Dates:

Pre-1950	1950-59	1960-69	1970-79	1980-85	1986-present

Copyright Dates of Materials Used:

Inappropriate   Appropriate

1	2	3	4	5

Research Level Indicated by Thesis:

Fact-finding	Asking/ Searching	Examining/ Organizing	Evaluating/ Deliberating	Integrating/ Concluding	Conceptualizing

Quality of Evidence:

Poor   Excellent

1	2	3	4	5

Quality of Conclusions:

Poor   Excellent

1	2	3	4	5

BIBLIOGRAPHY

Bowen, Ezra. "Can Colleges Teach Thinking?" *Time*, 16 February 1987, 61.

Brand, David. "The New Whiz Kids." *Time*, 31 August 1987, 42-51.

Buckley, Marilyn Hanf, and Owen Boyle. *Mapping the Writing Journey*. Berkeley, Calif.: University of California, Bay Area Writing Project, Curriculum Publication No. 15: 1-38, 1981. ERIC ED 225 191.

Costa, Arthur L. "The Principal's Role in Enhancing Thinking Skills." In *Developing Minds: A Resource Book for Teaching Thinking*, edited by Arthur L. Costa. Alexandria, Va.: Association for Supervision and Curriculum Development, 1985.

Critical Thinking A: Scholastic Social Studies Skills. New York: Scholastic, Inc., 1978. Teaching guide, transparencies, spirit masters.

Critical Thinking B: Scholastic Social Studies Skills. New York: Scholastic, Inc., 1980. Teaching guide, transparencies, spirit masters.

Elbow, Peter. *Writing with Power*. New York: Oxford University Press, 1981.

Ellis, Grace W. "Combining Invention and Design: Or Helping Students Plan before They Write." *Teaching English in the Two-Year College* 9 (Spring 1983): 219-26.

Gibaldi, Joseph, and Walter S. Achtert. *MLA Handbook for Writers of Research Papers, Theses, and Dissertations*. New York: Modern Language Association, 1977.

Graner, Michael H. "Revision Workshops: An Alternative to Peer Editing Groups." *English Journal* 76 (March 1987): 40-45.

Hubbard, Philip. *Alternative Outlining Techniques for ESL Composition.* CATESOL Occasional Papers, No. 10 (Fall 1984): 59-68. ERIC ED 253 065.

Kelly, Rebecca. *Meandering Roadways vs. Superhighways: An Approach to Teaching the Research Process.* Paper presented at the Annual Meeting of the Conference on College Composition and Communication (36th Minneapolis, Minn., March 21-23, 1985). ERIC ED 255 948.

Lamm, Kathryn. *10,000 Ideas for Term Papers, Projects and Reports.* New York: Arco Publishing, Inc., 1984.

Nickerson, Raymond S. "Why Teach Thinking?" In *Teaching Thinking Skills: Theory and Practice,* edited by Joan Boykoff Baron and Robert J. Sternberg. New York: W. H. Freeman and Company, 1987.

Opposing Viewpoints series. St. Paul, Minn.: Greenhaven Press, variable.

Perkins, D. N. "Thinking Frames: An Integrative Perspective on Teaching Cognitive Skills." In *Teaching Thinking Skills: Theory and Practice,* edited by Joan Boykoff Baron and Robert J. Sternberg. New York: W. H. Freeman and Company, 1987.

Powell, David. *What Can I Write About? 7000 Topics for High School Students.* Urbana, Ill.: National Council of Teachers of English, 1981.

Rico, Gabriele Lussar. *Writing the Natural Way: Using Right-Brain Techniques to Release Your Expressive Powers.* Los Angeles: J. P. Tarcher, Inc., 1983.

Schaffer, Jane. "When Students Ask Questions." *Academic Connections* (Winter 1987): 8-11.

Williams, Linda Verlee. *Teaching for the Two-Sided Mind: A Guide to Right Brain/Left Brain Education.* Englewood Cliffs, N.J.: Prentice-Hall, 1983.

Wolf, Dennis Palmer. "The Art of Questioning." *Academic Connections* (Winter 1987): 6-7.

INDEX